ATLA Monograph Series
edited by Dr. Kenneth E. Rowe

1. Ronald L. Grimes. *The Divine Imagination: William Blake's Major Prophetic Visions.* 1972.
2. George D. Kelsey. *Social Ethics Among Southern Baptists, 1917-1969.* 1973.
3. Hilda Adam Kring. *The Harmonists: A Folk-Cultural Approach.* 1973.
4. J. Steven O'Malley. *Pilgrimage of Faith: The Legacy of the Otterbeins.* 1973.
5. Charles Edwin Jones. *Perfectionist Persuasion: The Holiness Movement and American Methodism, 1867-1936.* 1974.
6. Donald E. Byrne, Jr. *No Foot of Land: Folklore of American Methodist Itinerants.* 1975.
7. Milton C. Sernett. *Black Religion and American Evangelicalism: White Protestants, Plantation Missions, and the Flowering of Negro Christianity, 1787-1865.* 1975.
8. Eva Fleischner. *Judaism in German Christian Theology Since 1945: Christianity and Israel Considered in Terms of Mission.* 1975.
9. Walter James Lowe. *Mystery & The Unconscious: A Study on the Thought of Paul Ricoeur.* 1977.
10. Norris Magnuson. *Salvation in the Slums: Evangelical Social Welfare Work, 1865-1920.* 1977.
11. William Sherman Minor. *Creativity in Henry Nelson Wieman.* 1977.
12. Thomas Virgil Peterson. *Ham and Japheth: The Mythic World of Whites in the Antebellum South.* 1978.
13. Randall K. Burkett. *Garveyism as a Religious Movement: The Institutionalization of a Black Civil Religion.* 1978.
14. Roger G. Betsworth. *The Radical Movement of the 1960's.* 1980.
15. Alice Cowan Cochran. *Miners, Merchants, and Missionaries: The Roles of Missionaries and Pioneer Churches in the Colorado Gold Rush and Its Aftermath, 1858-1870.* 1980.
16. Irene Lawrence. *Linguistics and Theology: The Significance of Noam Chomsky for Theological Construction.* 1980.

LINGUISTICS AND THEOLOGY

The Significance of Noam Chomsky for Theological Construction

Irene Lawrence

ATLA Monograph Series, No. 16

The Scarecrow Press, Inc. &
The American Theological Library Association
Metuchen, N.J., & London
1980

Library of Congress Cataloging in Publication Data

Lawrence, Irene, 1942-
   Linguistics and theology.

   (ATLA monograph series ; no. 16)
   Bibliography: p.
   Includes index.
   1. Christianity and language--History of
doctrines--20th century. 2. Chomsky, Noam.
I. Title. II. Series: American Theological
Library Association. ATLA monograph series ;
no. 16.
BR115.L25L38   230'.014   80-24210
ISBN 0-8108-1347-5

TABLE OF CONTENTS

EDITOR'S NOTE

Since 1972 the American Theological Library Association has
undertaken responsibility for a modest dissertation series in
the field of religious studies. Our aim in this series is to
publish two dissertations of quality each year at a reasonable
cost. Titles are selected from studies in a wide variety of
religious and theological disciplines nominated by graduate
school deans and directors of graduate studies. We are
pleased to publish Irene Lawrence's insightful study of Noam
Chomsky as number 16 in our series.

Following undergraduate studies in mathematics at
Stanford University, Professor Lawrence served as a mis-
sionary of the Episcopal Church in Liberia, West Africa,
where, in addition to teaching, she became Principal of the
House of Bethany in Robertsport. Returning to the United
States to study theology at the Church Divinity School of the
Pacific, Berkeley, she received the Master of Divinity degree
with distinction. She then took the doctorate in theology and
language at the Graduate Theological Union in Berkeley, the
first woman Episcopal Church Foundation Fellow to receive
the doctorate. Professor Lawrence is currently a member
of the religious studies faculty of the University of California at Davis and is editor for the Center for Hermeneutical
Studies in Berkeley.

Kenneth E. Rowe   Drew University Library
Series Editor   Madison, New Jersey 07940

v

FOREWORD

by Edward C. Hobbs

Noam Chomsky is one of that very small number of thinkers
whose thinking may rightly be called "revolutionary," that is,
initiating a revolution in our ways of thinking about fundamental matters. His field of research is styled "linguistics,"
usually regarded as a rather esoteric discipline, hardly likely to disturb settled ways of thinking in better-known fields
of human inquiry. Yet Chomsky's work has had an effect
much like that of Einstein's, shaking the foundations of discipline after discipline and inciting new modes of thinking in
those fields. Philosophy, psychology, and anthropology, no
less than linguistics, have felt the effect of Chomsky's thinking. He is truly a seminal thinker, one whose challenge to
the fundamental orientation of a science or sciences leads to
a new paradigm or model.

Should this revolution have any effect on theology?
Theology has always tended to go to philosophy for its paradigms, though in recent years there has been an opening toward other fields. But philosophy itself has been challenged
with respect to its paradigms by Chomsky's revolution; and
further, theology has always been a linguistic discipline if it

has been anything at all, a fact that might at least suggest some interest in what has happened in linguistic theory proper. Christian theology has generally been slow in appropriating scientific revolutions, waiting until they are forced upon it rather than engaging in an interested exploration in the bloom of the revolution's youth. Might it not be different this time, with theology in the midst of the struggle, rather than trailing far in the rear? Indeed it might!

Dr. Irene Lawrence has produced a remarkable guide to the possibility of utilizing Noam Chomsky's revolutionary work in the field of theology. In <u>Linguistics and Theology</u> she has kept her eye on her audience (namely, theologians and students of theology), and thus has not assumed a knowledge of the field of linguistics on the part of the reader, much less a knowledge of the intricacies of Chomsky's work. She presents us with a miniature history of the field of linguistics prior to Chomsky, in the course of a single chapter, which will orient the first-time visitor to the landmarks in that curious country sufficiently to grasp the revolutionary character of Chomsky's arrival on the scene. She then proceeds to give an introduction to Chomsky's linguistics, from its beginnings to its present elegance and complexity, which is the finest, clearest, and most accurate presentation of Chomsky's work known to me in any smaller compass than an entire book.

The impact of Chomsky's work on various fields would be a useful promise and/or warning to theologians; to this end, Dr. Lawrence has considered the interaction with behaviorist psychology, with linguistic philosophy, and with the now-altered field of linguistics itself. The antagonists are formidable ones indeed: such giants as B. F. Skinner in psychology and John Searle in philosophy; her analysis provides insight into the issues and their presuppositions in a clear and fair manner.

Having prepared the reader for such new terrain for exploration and discovery, the book now examines two significant theological issues of our time: pluralism and God-language. These are test-cases: if the proposed methodology works here, it might work anywhere in the discipline. Her contention is not that this approach to doing theology should eliminate all other methods, but rather that this method will shed new light on our theological questions and

vii

problems, that it will do some things better than other methods do, and perhaps even do some things that other methods cannot do.

Does her analysis show this? Only the reader can decide on that. Those who have examined her work prior to publication have found it compelling indeed, and as a delightful bonus, lucid. To discover that the obscurities and complexities of the work of Asa Kasher on mood implicatures can be translated into ordinary English sentences is refreshing indeed, especially if one is intimidated by strings of mathematical-style symbols. Irene Lawrence's undergraduate specialization was in mathematics, a background that no doubt prevented her being intimidated and that also no doubt assisted her in initiating the math-shy reader into the underlying simplicity of Kasher's argument. This lucidity extends also to her treatment of other less-known thinkers' works.

Her book is very much a programmatic essay: if taken seriously, it will function as a call to begin the task of theological construction along lines not hitherto utilized, a task that will need to be done in branch after branch of theology, with one problem after another examined with a new set of lenses as a prelude to beginning new construction in such problem areas and branches. Whether it will seem worth doing will depend in part on how well she has made her case in this book; but it will also depend on how open we are to beginning to do theology anew, on how willing we are to venture into unknown territory as a New World in which to seek, discover, explore, and celebrate that ultimacy which has no name and many names, whose surprisingness we bless to the end of the ages.

For the willing reader, a delightful adventure lies ahead in the reading of this book!

Berkeley, California
February 1980

ACKNOWLEDGMENTS

Few, if any, works of scholarship spring full-grown from their creators' minds, and certainly not this one. In its first incarnation as a dissertation, this book was made possible by an unusually helpful and enthusiastic thesis committee and adviser. My thanks go to Professor Benjamin A. Reist of the San Francisco Theological Seminary and the Graduate Theological Union, who at short notice gave his time and assistance with great generosity. My thanks go also to Professor Kevin A. Wall, O.P., of the Dominican School of Philosophy and Theology and the Graduate Theological Union, who helped and encouraged me through some of the puzzling intricacies of scholastic philosophy. I am deeply grateful to Professor Julian C. Boyd of the University of California at Berkeley, who guided me through all my doctoral study. Besides giving me the benefits of his knowledge and his enthusiastic support, it was his work on modals that led to the idea that has now emerged as this book. Finally, my deepest thanks and gratitude go to my adviser, Professor Edward C. Hobbs of the Church Divinity School of the Pacific and the Graduate Theological Union. Professor Hobbs taught me, advised me, and occasionally fought for me for seven years and through two degrees; my debt to him is enormous, and he will always be the model of teacher, scholar, and friend for me.

ix

Another person I wish to thank is Noam Chomsky, both for making this project possible in the most significant sense and for the kind interest he showed in the project during the two weeks (8-18 January 1979) he was giving the Immanuel Kant Lectures at Stanford University.

I am also grateful to those who showed their confidence in me by helping me financially during my studies. The Episcopal Church Foundation awarded me fellowship grants for three years, the first of which (1975-76) was the William B. Given, Jr., Memorial Fellowship established by the Arthur Vining Davis Foundations. An earlier generous gift from Mr. Thomas W. Cummings created the Hellenistic Greek Linguistics Project of the Center for Hermeneutical Studies of the Graduate Theological Union and the University of California at Berkeley. His gift and a matching grant from I. B. M. made possible a year's research on this project.

My thanks go also to the Church Divinity School of the Pacific for appointing me Teaching Fellow during the two years I was writing what has become this book; to the Reverend Esther H. Davis, for beautifully typing the original manuscript; and to Dean Claude Welch of the Graduate Theological Union for bringing this work to the attention of the American Theological Library Association.

I gratefully acknowledge permission to use quotations from these works:

Aspects of the Theory of Syntax, by Noam Chomsky, is used by permission of M. I. T. Press. Copyright © 1965 by the Massachusetts Institute of Technology.

Reflections on Language, by Noam Chomsky, is used by permission of Pantheon Books, a Division of Random House, Inc. Copyright © 1975 by Noam Chomsky.

The Logical Structure of Linguistic Theory, by Noam Chomsky, is used by permission of Plenum Publishing Corporation. Copyright © 1975 by Noam Chomsky.

Theology of the New Testament, Vol. II, by Rudolf Bultmann, translated by Kendrick Grobel, is used by permission of Charles Scribner's Sons and of SCM Press.

PREFACE

This book is yet one more in the series of attempts to come
to an understanding of Christian faith in the modern world.
Many, if not a majority, of twentieth-century theologians have
wrestled with the problem in one way or another; various
ways of bridging the apparent gulf fixed between Christianity
and modern life have been proposed. Some insist that the
world must change; some call for better communication; some
want to make Christianity "relevant" by abandoning this or
that archaic dogma or institutional structure; some try to
"translate" old conceptualities into new ones; and a few
demand the abolition of Christianity itself in the name of
Christ. Some of these movements are mentioned in the following pages; many have provided valuable insights, but none
has been completely successful.

My introduction to the magnitude of the problem occurred when I found myself teaching religious studies to
junior and senior high school students. I had assumed that
there would be much ignorance, some acceptance, and a fair
amount of rejection of Christianity among my students; what
I had not expected was that my students had, over the years,
learned reasonably well how to talk a fairly "correct," inter-
nally consistent, system of Christianity. On the whole, they

were perfectly sincere about it, and yet, on the whole, they did not expect this way of talking to have the slightest effect on their lives outside the church and the religious studies classroom. It was the irrelevance of the beliefs to anything that they considered important, coupled with the sincerity with which they held the beliefs, that opened my eyes. No one sees so well as the once-blind, and over the intervening years I have felt this dislocation in more and more places, including some that deeply touch my own life.

This work is, in a sense, the heir of the various translational approaches that preceded it, enriched by the much deeper understanding of the whole translational process available now, provided largely by Noam Chomsky's Transformational-Generative Linguistics. It would be impossible to use this preface to tell the reader what the book says; for better or for worse, the book itself must do that. But it might be useful to mention here something that this book is not about, if only to avoid disappointment.

Although I mention some theologians who have attempted to deal with the same subject in terms of the special character of religious language, this book is not about religious language. No matter how broadly "religious" may be defined, if it is to be a useful concept there must be, at least potentially, something outside its bounds, something that can be characterized as nonreligious. The gulf will enter there again. Some well-intentioned theologians wish to expand the sphere of the religious to include all of human life. At that point, it seems to me, the word "religious" becomes superfluous, and we might just as well speak simply of human life--or of human language, in this case.

I hope that this work may be of interest to linguists as well as theologians, and therefore I have tried not to assume a knowledge of the one field on the part of practitioners of the other. Thus the theologian will find an explanation of the linguistic models involved, and the linguist will find a discussion of the theological issues. Although of course I speak mainly for theologians, co-operation between our two fields would seem to promise highly desirable results. I offer this beginning attempt to investigate the potential promise to all who are willing to test new modes of construction for some old problems.

xiii

INTRODUCTION

Theology has always found expression in some conceptual system, usually that of the prevailing mode or modes of thought
of the theologian's time.   But modes of thought and conceptualities change, and the creative constructive theologians
were those who were able to use new (or newly-at-hand) conceptual systems for their theological work, thus opening up
new ways of doing theology for their successors.   Augustine,
for example, made Neo-Platonism available for theology, and
Aquinas did the same for the rediscovered Aristotle.

        While it is clear to many people in the twentieth cen-
tury that the old theological systems have broken down, it is
not at all clear what (if anything) is to replace them.   Many
twentieth-century constructive theologians have attempted to
develop new ways of doing theology; some of them have been
influential, but none are universally accepted.   Thus there is
a continued need for investigation into the possible usefulness
of new intellectual systems for constructive theology.

        In this work I investigate one such new intel-
lectual system, the one usually called transformational-
generative linguistics, as it has been developed by Noam
Chomsky, together with his concomitant theory of language
and mind.   And I make some proposals as to how it may be

useful for theological work by applying it to two of the major theological problems of our present situation, pluralism and God-language. Chomsky's work has already had important effects in fields outside that of pure linguistics--for example, in psychology, philosophy, and anthropology and ethnography. It seems particularly plausible that it would be helpful in theology, since theology is primarily a linguistic discipline, always expressing itself in language. Therefore a new theory of language could have profound effects on theology; and toward that goal is directed this essay on its importance and its possibility.

Chapter I

LINGUISTICS BEFORE CHOMSKY

Pre-Nineteenth Century

In Western culture the systematic study of language--as of
so many other fields--began in classical Greece. The solu-
tions developed for Greek and then extended to Latin were
the basis for the linguistics of the Western world until tho
nineteenth century, and, in some respects, until the twentieth.
What we now distinguish as philosophy of language and linguistics were, of course, not considered separable disciplines
by the Greeks, and so one of the earliest discussions of the
nature of language that we have, Plato's Cratylus, [1] deals
with whether language is arbitrary, that is, merely conventional, or whether it corresponds in some way to reality.
One of the participants in the dialogue is Cratylus, who (supported by Socrates, at least for the sake of the argument)
says that there is indeed an "inherent correctness in names,
which is the same for all men, both Greeks and barbarians, "
and that a name indicates "the essential nature of each thing
by means of letters and syllables. "[2] Plato's discussion here
is carried out in terms of names and things named (referents);
this understanding of language as referential, as somehow corresponding to reality, prevailed, with varying degrees of

1

sophistication, through the early twentieth century in the philosophy of language; the first philosophy of language that explicitly rejected this understanding was the post-Tractatus work of Ludwig Wittgenstein. [3]

The method used in the Cratylus to show the natural connection between words and reality was etymology. The origin of a word was its "true" (ἔτυμος , true) meaning. Etymological investigations led to the attempt to sort out and classify different kinds of words and the relationships between them. Those grammarians who emphasized the regularity in Greek came to be called analogists (from ἀναλογία, proportion, relation); those who emphasized the irregularities were called anomalists (from ἀνωμαλία , unevenness, irregularity). The anomalists were, on the whole, supporters of the naturalist interpretation of language; they claimed that if language were merely conventional, it would be much more regular than in fact it is. It is language's "natural" correspondence with reality that blocks complete regularity. Thus the irregular facts of language are important in their own right.

In the midst of this discussion, the particular details of classical grammar began to be hammered out. Protagoras, a fifth-century Sophist, first distinguished the three genders in Greek (although the names "masculine," "feminine," and "neuter" did not settle down until later). Plato first distinguished nouns and verbs as logical categories (not grammatical categories); what we now call adjectives were included under verbs. Aristotle added "conjunctions"--everything that was neither a noun nor a verb in Plato's sense. Later Greeks moved adjectives to the noun class. Aristotle also recognized what we now call tense in a verb, although he disastrously linked it with temporality. The Stoics distinguished the article and proper and common nouns as parts of speech; they also developed the notions of case for nouns, and, for verbs, aspect (complete or not), voice (active or passive), and the distinction between transitive and intransitive.

After the city of Alexandria became a major center of Greek scholarship, grammar was codified. In the second century B. C. Dionysius Thrax wrote the first comprehensive grammar. He added adverbs, participles, pronouns, and prepositions to the parts of speech, but did not discuss syntax. That was first done for Greek by Apollonius Dyscolus in the second century A. D.

The Alexandrian scholars also established what Lyons[4] calls the "classical fallacy" in the study of language.[5] It has two parts. First, the Alexandrian grammarians--in fact all the previous Greek scholars of language--were principally concerned with literary works and thus took the written language as primary. The distinction between written and spoken language was rarely made, and, when it was made, the spoken language was thought to derive from the written. Second, again partly because of the Alexandrians' literary concern, the language of the "Golden Age," the age of the fifth-century Athenian writers, was considered "correct," and contemporary colloquial speech was "corrupt." This is the origin of the notion, which is still alive in many circles today, that one function of grammar is prescriptive; it prescribes how language ought to be used on the basis of some absolute and "pure" form of the language.

Latin grammarians copied the Greek models in both form and content. Since Latin is in many surface respects similar to Greek, only minor changes had to be made to regard the details of the Greek solution as universal categories, which could be applied to all languages. The grammarians of the Middle Ages cleaned up a few more grammatical details--for example, they finished the development of the traditional parts of speech. They also regarded the written language as primary, partly because of the status of Latin as a now-foreign language, primarily written but culturally very important. They also explicitly and philosophically developed the notion that all languages have the same parts of speech and other grammatical categories and are thus able to express the same concepts. Roger Bacon said, "Grammar is substantially the same in all languages, even though it may vary accidentally."[6]

The Renaissance humanists revived the study of the classical languages, and at the same time revived (if indeed it had ever really weakened) the Alexandrian "classical fallacy." Language was studied as the language of literature, and this "good" language was held up as the standard. For example, Cicero, not medieval Latin, was correct Latin. As the study of the European vernaculars began and developed, the same principles were applied to them. And the categories and principles developed for Greek and very slightly modified for Latin were imposed on the vernaculars. This forced, for example, the "predicate nominative" onto English as the "correct" form (It's I), instead of the native "predicate objective" (It's me) of past and present usage.

In a sense, the famous Port-Royal grammar of 1660, Gram-maire générale et raisonnée, was still within the classical tra-dition in its claim of a universal structure common to all languages.[7]

The Nineteenth Century: Historical Linguistics and Comparative Philology

By the nineteenth century that change in understanding that we loosely call "the rise of the modern world view" had replaced the classical world view. Reasoning from abstract principles as the primary explanatory method gave way to scientific and historical reasoning, which produces explana-tions in terms of inductive hypotheses and developmental or evolutionary theories. This move started with the natural sciences, but was gradually applied to other disciplines. One of the precipitating factors for its application to the study of language was the gradual increase in the information availa-ble about various languages, including more non-European languages. Of particular importance was the discovery of Sanskrit and its grammatical tradition.

The Sanskrit tradition is older than the Greek; its most famous representative, Pāṇini, worked in the fourth century B.C., but refers to a long tradition before him. Sanskrit was a language with such pronounced resemblances to Greek and Latin that they could not be accidental. Of course, it had always been clear that Greek and Latin were similar to each other, but their resemblances could be ex-plained by their many and close associations. Now scholars were presented with a language whose similarities to Greek and Latin could not be explained by cultural cross-borrowing. The hypothesis of a common origin was made as early as 1786 by Sir William Jones, who had spent some time as Chief Justice in Bengal, but the nineteenth century developed theo-ries of language change and genetic relationship that put this hypothesis on a sound scientific basis. The description of the extent and structure of the Indo-European family was the fruit of this approach, as was the classification of many other language families, for example, Semitic, Algonquian, and Sino-Tibetan. This period in linguistics, roughly correspond-ing to the nineteenth century, is called "comparative philology" or "historical linguistics."

One of the achievements of comparative philology was the sharpening of the vague idea of similarity into the precise

"systematic correspondence." This began with phonetic correspondences. Philologists formulated, for example, sound-
shift rules to describe the systematic sound changes that took
place in the historical phonetic development of each language
family. This often involved hypothesizing intermediate stages
that had to be reconstructed--"Proto-Germanic," for example,
or "Proto-Indo-European" as the parent language of the whole
family. The model for this, of course, was Latin's relation
to the Romance languages, an unusual case only in that copi-
ous documentation existed in both the mother and the daugh-
ter languages. Elements of language other than sound were
also investigated in this manner, for example, conjugation
systems, but comparative philology was particularly successful in analyzing sound laws. The most famous such sound
law, although not the first, is called Grimm's law, after
Jakob Grimm, who formulated a version of it in 1822.[8]

Those of Grimm's generation were not worried about
the many exceptions of their rules of sound shift; they expected these "laws" to apply to the majority of cases, but
thought that some random words, or sounds within words,
for example, would be skipped over by the shift and retain
their earlier form. However, in the last quarter or so of
the nineteenth century a new generation of comparative philologists began to assert that the sound laws are, or at
least should be, without exception. If they were only properly formulated, they would apply across the board. Some
satisfactory explanation--say, borrowing--must be provided
for all apparent exceptions, and such an explanation is always available if all relevant factors can be taken into account. This group of philologists came to be called the
Junggrammatiker ("young grammarians," or "neo-grammar-
ians"). For example, a number of apparent exceptions to
Grimm's Law are no longer exceptions if the original accent
is taken into account; this 1875 addition to Grimm's Law was
formulated by Karl Verner.[9]

Besides this principle of regularity the Junggrammatiker also established the principle of analogy to explain
systematic language changes. Languages, they said, tend
to create new forms by analogy to already existing forms.
An English example of analogy in spelling is the insertion of
"l" in "could" by analogy to the "l's" that were regularly in
"should" and "would." An example of an analogy that has
not succeeded in English is speak-speaked paralleling walk-
walked. Early grammarians had considered this process
one of the things that corrupted a language and that it was

their duty to correct; they always spoke of "false analogy."
The Junggrammatiker recognized that it was a constant factor in the development of languages.

During this period the "classical fallacy" was greatly
weakened, but not altogether eliminated. Because of the
comparative philologists' historical interests, they had their
greatest successes with language families with written records
spanning the centuries. This is one reason for the fuller
picture of Indo-European, as compared with other language
families. But comparative philology explained changes in
the available written evidence on the basis of sound shifts,
thus paving the way for the later explicit recognition that
the spoken language is primary. Similarly, the ground was
laid for the rejection of the theory that there was a pure
literary language with various substandard "dialects," although major studies of dialects did not begin until close to
the twentieth century. When dialect study was begun it
was undertaken partly in opposition to the Junggrammatiker,
to show that much more than simple sound development was
at work in language change. In general a so-called "standard language" can be shown to be merely a "dialect" that
has become important for nonlinguistic reasons--usually political and economic reasons. Thus the distinction between
"correct" and "corrupt" language was blurred by the appreciation of the fact that all languages change constantly, and
the notion of "prescriptive" grammar was correspondingly
weakened.

Before we leave the nineteenth century there is one
other factor to consider, which, although it did not greatly
influence nineteenth-century linguistics, was important for
the development of twentieth-century structural linguistics.
During the nineteenth century for the first time many Euro-
peans--missionaries and colonial officers in Africa, Asia,
and Oceania--had to cope with unwritten languages. Many of
the Europeans reached a high degree of competence in these
new languages, and many of them wrote textbooks and dic-
tionaries to help others learn the language. Most such attempts at grammar followed the traditional, classical patterns their writers had learned for European languages, but
a few found that their new languages did not fit easily into
the old procrustean bed and resisted the temptation to distort
them to fit. This emancipation from what had been thought
to be universal grammatical categories and the consequent
rejection of any boundaries on possible languages in the
name of a description based on field experience were to

become a leading characteristic of the next stage of linguistic inquiry, structural linguistics.

European Structuralism: Ferdinand de Saussure

Ferdinand de Saussure was a Swiss scholar, who taught at the University of Paris and then the University of Geneva. From 1906 to 1911 he taught three courses in general linguistics in Geneva. He did not publish much during his lifetime--his major work, a treatise on the Proto-Indo-European vocalic system, was published while he was still a student. Yet what he was interested in was the structure or patterns of language as a whole, into which the individual facts studied by the comparative philologist would fit. He finally began teaching his new ideas at the University of Geneva, causing considerable excitement among his students. After his death in 1913 some of his students hoped to publish his lecture notes or outlines for the benefit of those who had not taken his courses; they found that de Saussure had not kept any drafts of the lectures. So, with the few personal notes of de Saussure that they could find, and with the class notes taken by several students during the three courses, the two editors did their best to reconstruct his thought. The result was published in 1915 as Cours de linguistique générale.[10]

De Saussure drew at least two distinctions that have had a major influence on subsequent linguistics. The first is the distinction between la langue and la parole. La langue is the collective pattern of a language, a self-contained whole. It is those "speech facts" that are not under the control of the individual speaker. La parole, on the other hand, is always a particular act performed by an individual. La langue "exists in the form of a sum of impressions deposited in the brain of each member of a community, almost like a dictionary of which identical copies have been distributed to each individual." La parole is "the sum of what people say."[11] La langue and la parole cannot be studied at the same time or by the same methods, and the object of linguistics is la langue only. (In the rest of this section the English word "language" will be used for de Saussure's la langue, and "speaking" for la parole.) This distinction between language and speaking is natural and not arbitrary; under certain circumstances a person can lose the ability to speak and yet retain language, and dead languages, which are no longer spoken, can be learned.

The second enduring distinction that de Saussure made was between two different ways of studying language. Linguistics, as a science, has to cope with something that most other sciences do not have to consider: the effects of time on its object, language. The part of linguistics that studies the changes over time of a language de Saussure proposes to call evolutionary, or diachronic linguistics. This, of course, was the type of linguistics that preoccupied the nineteenth century. However, as de Saussure pointed out, a person uses language consistently without being aware of the evolutionary history of the items that make up the language. A word, for example, may have come into a language as a loan word, borrowed from another language; but when it is used in its new language it has become a part of the system of that language. At any particular time the state of a language at that time can be studied and described; this is static or synchronic linguistics. Both types of linguistics are useful and necessary, and both are covered in de Saussure's Course (in fact, the section on diachronic linguistics is slightly longer than the section on synchronic linguistics). The important thing is not to confuse the two, or the methods appropriate to each.

De Saussure pictures the relationships among the elements of a language state as falling into two groups or dimensions. Language as produced is intrinsically linear; therefore any given element is related to the elements that precede or follow it. De Saussure called this linear dimension of relationship "syntagmatic." Syntagmatic relationships include, on one level, syntax--for example, the grammatical relationship noun and verb in a particular sentence would be a syntagmatic relation. But syntagms cover all serial relations, not just syntax. The other dimension of relations includes all the nonlinear associations that words have or acquire; therefore, de Saussure called these "associative relations." Generally one cannot predict either the number or the order of the terms in an associative series, since they depend upon mental association. De Saussure gives the example shown on page 9.

One type of associative series is the inflectional paradigm, or grammatical paradigms in general. In such cases the number of terms is definite, but the order of their occurrence is still random. De Saussure's examples are Latin "dominus, dominī, dominō, etc., ... obviously an associative group formed around a common element, the noun theme

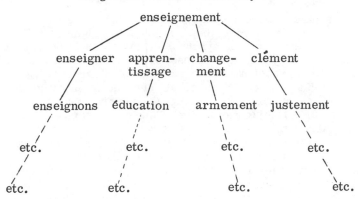

domin-" and, in French on a different level, the "latent syntactical pattern" que vous dit-il?, que te dit-il?, que nous
dit-il?[13] Because of the importance of this type of associative relation, later linguists, following a 1936 suggestion by
L. Hjelmslev, renamed it the "paradigmatic relation."[14]
Since de Saussure, structural linguistics has used the de
Saussurean distinction between syntagmatic and paradigmatic
to study the structural relations at any given level of a language. For example, at the phonological level, the study of
the distinctive contrasting consonant and vowel elements of
a particular language is a paradigmatic study, while the study
of the possible syllable structures--what consonants are allowed to combine, for example--is syntagmatic.

In at least two other respects de Saussure was the
first modern linguist. First, he insisted explicitly that
spoken language is primary, and written language, although
indispensable, is secondary. Writing, said de Saussure,
exists for the sole purpose of representing the spoken lan-
guage--or, to be exact, of representing language. The representation is far from perfect, due to the inadequacies of
the alphabet and to the fact that writing tends to be conservative; pronunciation and language use tend to change faster
than writing, so writing often represents an archaic system.
Unfortunately, the greater the discrepancy between writing
and language, the greater the temptation to take writing as
the standard, especially when the language change is regarded
as corruption. Modern linguists, following de Saussure, universally accept the primacy of the spoken language.

Related to this is the question of what language is
"correct" and, in particular, whether the role of the linguist

is to legislate correct usage. For de Saussure the function
of linguistics is to describe, not to pass judgment. One may
speak, for example, of synchronic "laws," but they are not
imperative; they simply express what arrangements actually
exist. To think of a particular state of a language as having a special status, to which all subsequent language must
conform, is an illusion. "Language never errs; it simply
takes a different viewpoint."[15] This conception of linguistics
as a science that explains what language is, not what it ought
to be, is often expressed by the label "descriptive" linguistics, as contrasted with "prescriptive" linguistics. Twentieth-
century linguistics is uniformly descriptive. "Descriptive"
linguistics also contrasts with historical linguistics, and in
this sense also twentieth-century linguistics is largely descriptive. However, historical linguistics is not rejected as
improper in the way that prescriptive linguistics is. In this
second sense, also, de Saussure's synchronic linguistics was
descriptive.

American Structuralism

Structuralism in the United States came to accept and
use most of the distinctions made by de Saussure, but early
twentieth-century American linguistics had a flavor all its
own because of its major motivation: the need to investigate
and record the rapidly disappearing American Indian languages.
In the absence of any significant written records, at least for
the languages within the United States--American Indian alpha-
bets were developed only after exposure to European writing
--the diachronic dimension of investigation was confined to
the establishment of a few language families. Most linguists'
efforts were concentrated on describing the existing state of
whatever language they were investigating; the heavy emphasis on fieldwork and the goal of producing grammars of previously unknown languages were characteristic of American
linguistics of this period. In fact, it is sometimes called
anthropological linguistics.

The pioneer of American structural linguistics was
Franz Boas, who in 1899 became the first professor of anthropology at Columbia University. He and his students did
intensive and detailed fieldwork, collecting quantities of facts,
usually from informants, but being somewhat cautious in
making generalizations from the data. Boas standardized
phonetic notation, and insisted upon very careful attention to
the smallest variations in detail of pronunciation, even at the
cost of very complex data.

One of Boas's first students was Edward Sapir, who shared Boas's passion for careful fieldwork, but who was more interested in synthesizing the data into a comprehensive theory. When the theory of the phoneme became available Sapir and his followers adopted it to describe the sound system of a language, whereas Boas continued to describe each detail. Both Boas and Sapir, however, in their different ways, believed that the necessary starting point in linguistic description was the sound system of a language. That only speech is properly language became a dogma of structuralist linguistics.

Sapir's most influential work was a popularization, Language, published in 1921.[16] Unlike Boas, Sapir was interested in the external relationships of language; he discusses, among other things, language and race, geography, psychology, and literature. However, he does not neglect language per se. He discusses first the elements of speech: "The true, significant elements of language are generally sequences of sounds that are either words, significant parts of words, or word groupings."[17] There are, roughly, two types of elements, "radical" elements (e.g., sing-) and "grammatical" elements (e.g., -ing, -er, -s). Grammatical elements include not only separable affixes, but such things as modification of the stem by a vowel change or by reduplication, and accent change. A grammatical element may even be a "zero" element, one that does not change the radical element. Any given language tends to use the same types of grammatical elements for all grammatical functions, and, usually, more than one type for the same function. For example, both suffix (-ed) and stem vowel change are used for English "past tense." Sapir concludes that "linguistic form may and should be studied as types of patterning, apart from the associated functions."[18]

This direction of analysis led to the development of the idea "morpheme," an analogy to phoneme on the word-formation level, although Sapir does not use either term in Language. A morpheme was the smallest distinctive unit of word formation, or, better, the smallest unit of grammatical analysis; its form might vary from word to word (as the English "past tense" morphemes above), and might not even be separable from the word (e.g., the "past tense" morpheme in went). As the theory of morphemes developed linguists were increasingly able to describe word formation in any given language, and two parts of grammar, morphology and phonology, were done with more and more success. What was usually considered the third part of grammar, syntax, was usually very sketchily described, and sometimes included under morphology.

Boas and Sapir were both important to the development of American structural linguistics, but the single most influential linguist was Leonard Bloomfield, whose 1933 work (also called Language[19]) was a summary and synthesis of the whole linguistic enterprise up to that time, plus many significant innovations of his own. The book became the standard textbook and reference work for American linguistics for at least twenty years. Bloomfield introduced many of the technical terms used in subsequent linguistics. For example, he introduces the term "immediate constituent" in these words:

> Any English-speaking person who concerns himself with this matter is sure to tell us that the immediate constituents of Poor John ran away are the two forms poor John and ran away; that each of these is, in turn, a complex form; that the immediate constituents of ran away are ran ... and away ...; and that the immediate constituents of poor John are ... poor and John.[20]

Bloomfield took an explicitly behaviorist approach in Language, although the only effect of his behaviorism was in his description of meaning, which he linked with stimulus and response. He described a supposedly typical situation:

> Suppose Jack and Jill are walking down a lane. Jill is hungry. She sees an apple in a tree. She makes a noise with her larynx, tongue, and lips. Jack vaults the fence, climbs the tree, takes the apple, brings it to Jill, and places it in her hand. Jill eats the apple.[21]

In Bloomfield's analysis the stimulus was Jill's being hungry and seeing the apple; all this is at least theoretically describable in terms of observable and measurable entities-- the secretion of gastric juices and the reflections of light waves, among many others. These are "the practical events preceding the event of speech." Jill could have made a direct response; she could have picked (or tried to pick) the apple herself. Instead she made a substitute response; she spoke. Her response (speech) was a stimulus to Jack, whose response was getting Jill the apple (the "practical events following the act of speech"). The fact of speech is unimportant in itself, but like other unimportant things it has a meaning because it is connected with important things--the "practical events." The meaning of Jill's speech, then, is the situation of stimulus and (direct) response, namely, the practical events preceding and following the utterance.[22] In theory, therefore, all speech can be completely explained in terms of stimulus and response; in practice, since we would need a complete description (including history) of everything involved in the stimulus, and this is obviously not possible, at least in our present stage of knowledge, the study of meaning is currently futile.

This barrier to the study of meaning, however, did not affect Bloomfield's study of phonology or morphology. All that was necessary in terms of meaning was being able to tell whether two phonetic or morphological forms were "the same" or "different." No scientific precision about meaning is needed. (Here again, the phoneme is the model for the morpheme.) Once the basic units of the language are established by pair tests or something of the kind, the rules for their possible combinations are to be stated in purely formal terms, without any reference to their meaning. This independence from semantics remained characteristic of Bloomfield's followers (that is, almost all American linguists for the next twenty years).

In later terminology the goal of the Bloomfieldians was described as the construction of a "discovery procedure," which, when applied to data from an unknown language, would produce the correct grammar of that language, in terms of its own structure, not based on Latin or Greek models. Instead of the traditional "parts of speech" the linguists looked for "substitution classes," whose members could replace each other in specified slots in sentences. The process of division of words and phrases into their appropriate classifications was done in terms of immediate constituents (immediate constituent analysis), and led to structural formulas for groups of sentences, each symbol of which represented a substitution class or possibly a morpheme.

To sum up, this period in American linguistics was characterized by several interrelated features, mostly stemming from the heavy interest in the study of American Indian languages. One was the insistence on fieldwork. Another was the acceptance of the primacy of speech over writing.

Another was the use of the phoneme and morpheme as basic units, and the rejection of meaning as a method of analysis. Another was the insistence that each language be described in its own terms, along with the presupposition that its own terms would not be those developed for Greek and Latin; the emphasis was on the great diversity of languages and the need to describe quickly and accurately the grammars of the many languages that were on the verge of extinction.

Early Transformational Theory: Zellig S. Harris

The most comprehensive example of a Bloomfieldian-type linguistics after Bloomfield himself and probably the most comprehensive effort ever to develop a "discovery procedure" for language was produced by Zellig S. Harris. His Methods of Structural Linguistics was published in 1951.[23] In it Harris attempted to offer procedures--not the only possible ones, he says--to arrange linguistic data to show the different structures of different languages. His procedures are divided into phonological and morphological procedures; some of what might be called syntactical is included under the morphological. In both phonology and morphology Harris intends to describe procedures for identifying the distinct elements of each (i.e., the phonemes and morphemes), and then to state the relations among the elements in distributional terms. Meaning is not to be involved except as "the linguist's and the layman's shortcut to a distributional differentiation. In principle, meaning need be involved only to the extent of determining what is repetition."[24]

Harris made explicit the operation of substitution for identifying "substitution classes" for both phonemes and morphemes; the advantage, of course, is the simplification of not having constantly to repeat distribution statements for almost identical morphemes. He explains that the procedure

> consists essentially of repeated substitution: e.g., child for young boy in where did the --- go? To generalize this, we take a form A in an environment C --- D and then substitute another form B in the place of A. If after such a substitution, we still have an expression which occurs in the language concerned, i.e., if not only CAD but also CBD occurs, we say that A and B are members of the same substitution class, or that both A and

B fill the position C --- D, or the like. The
operation of substitution is basic in descriptive
linguistics.[25]

Repeated substitution led to "parts of speech" that could be
defined in purely structural terms and yet preserved what
seemed intuitively significant in the traditional meaning-
based "parts of speech"; thus Harris and other structuralists
retained most of the traditional names for the newly defined
parts of speech. Now any number of sentences could be described with the same structural formula. If N is noun, V
verb, T article, and v tense and verb "auxiliary," the formula T N_1 v V T N_2 describes these sentences (and many
others):

The kids broke the window.
The detective will watch the staff.
The citizens destroyed the barracks.

In a 1957 article, "Co-occurrence and Transformation
in Linguistic Structure,"[26] Harris stated the first version
of an explicitly postdescriptive or poststructural linguistics
by adding a new level, which he called transformations, to
grammatical analysis. Harris had published a preliminary
list of English transformations as early as 1952,[27] and the
1957 article was actually delivered, in its essentials, in
1955. In order to define transformations Harris first defined
co-occurrence. For any two element classes in a particular
construction--say adjective (A) and noun (N) in English in the
English construction AN--"the A-co-occurrence of hopes (as
N) includes slight (slight hopes of peace) but probably not
green." The co-occurrences depend on the construction involved; "the N-co-occurrents of man (as N_i) in N_i is a N
may include organism, beast, development, searcher, while
the N-co-occurrents of man in N_i's N may include hopes,
development, imagination, etc."[28] In these two constructions
(N is a N, N's N) the co-occurrences are different. But in
many other pairs of constructions the co-occurrences are the
same (or almost the same); in such a case the constructions
are transforms of each other; that is, one was derived from
the other by a transformation. In the fourth section of the
article Harris lists all the major English transformations in
three groups. The first group consists of all transformations
that change an independent sentence into another independent
sentence. The second group is those that change an independent sentence into a sequential one, and the third group
nominalizes sentences. Harris uses a single-shafted arrow to

indicate a transformation, pointing both ways for a reversible transformation (↔) and one way for an irreversible transformation (→). An example of the first group, sentence to sentence (S↔S) is the passive transformation, symbolized by the structural formula N_1 v V N_2 → N_2 v be Ven by N_1. The independent active sentence (for example, the children were drinking milk) is transformed into an independent passive sentence (milk was being drunk by the children). The transformation is not reversible because some sentences that can be described as N_2 v be Ven by N_1--the wreck was seen by the seashore--do not have elements that can co-occur with elements of N_1 v V N_2. The second group (S1↔S2) includes sentence sequences using combiners of various sorts and "zero recurrence" of matched "introducers"--for example, the sequence Some people are cynical. Some are not.[29] The third group are nominalizations (S↔N), which usually involve verb form changes, such as replacing the v with to or -ing. Dogs bark is transformed into barking dogs (N $\overline{v}$ V ↔ Ving N), or Actors play the part becomes actors to play the part (N_1 v V N_2 → N_1 to V N_2).

Harris intended his list of transformations to be a list of elementary transformations; they may be combined in specific ways and in certain sequences to make all observed transformations. That means that for any given sentence, identification of all the transformations will lead to the identification of the underlying sentence or sentences and combiners that have been transformed. Harris calls this process "factorization." Sentences that are different will have different factorizations, but it is also possible that one sentence may have two or more different factorizations, since it is possible for two or more different underlying sentences to undergo different transformations and end up looking alike. (Compare barking dogs and reading plays.)

Harris calls the elementary underlying sentences kernel sentences; all the sentences of the language come from the kernel sentences and the combiners being acted upon by the transformations. The kernel sentences can be grouped into a very few constructions, so few, in fact, that the whole kernel of English grammar can be printed on half a page of Harris's article.[30] In general, descriptive linguistics worked best on analyses of the kernel area of grammar, since all sentences are supposed to have an immediate constituent analysis. With the addition of transforms, linguistics can abandon the search for constituent analysis where it does not exist and use transformational analysis instead. Harris remarks, "For this and other reasons a language cannot be fully described in purely constructional terms, without the transform relation."[31]

Noam Chomsky was a student of Harris's in both undergraduate and graduate work at the University of Pennsylvania. (John Lyons reports, "Chomsky himself has explained that it was really his sympathy with Harris's political views that led him to work as an undergraduate in linguistics."[32]) Harris thanks Chomsky for "much-needed assistance with the manuscript" of Structural Linguistics,[33] and in "Co-occurrence" he says,

> From a time when this work was still at an early stage, Noam Chomsky has been carrying out partly related studies of transformations and their position in linguistic analysis.... My many conversations with Chomsky have sharpened the work presented here, in addition to being a great pleasure in themselves.[34]

Chomsky for his part has had no hesitation in acknowledging his debts to Harris. In Syntactic Structures, published in the same year as Harris's article, he says,

> During the whole period of this research I have had the benefit of very frequent and lengthy discussions with Zellig S. Harris. So many of his ideas and suggestions are incorporated in the text below and in the research on which it is based that I will make no attempt to indicate them by special reference.[35]

The points of resemblance between "Co-occurrence" and Syntactic Structures can be seen, especially in the extent of their common vocabulary. Although the notions and the vocabulary have undergone a sea change in Syntactic Structures, making Chomsky (with all his indebtedness to Harris) the true author of the transformational-generative revolution, Harris, nevertheless, prepared the way.

Notes

[1]For the Cratylus I am using the Greek-English edition of the Loeb Classical Library (Plato, Vol. IV), trans. H. N. Fowler.

[2]Ibid. § 1, § 34.

[3]It may very well be the case that there were philosophers who worked out of a different understanding of language. But those who explicitly discussed language discussed it in referential terms. (The reconstruction of ancient linguistics presented here is the one prevailing in recent works on linguistics [cf. footnote 4]; other interpretations of the work of individual philosophers and theorists are of course both possible and actual.)

[4]For the history of linguistics through the nineteenth century I am indebted to the accounts in John Lyons, Introduction to Theoretical Linguistics (Cambridge: Cambridge University Press, 1971), pp. 4-38, and in H. A. Gleason, Linguistics and English Grammar (New York: Holt, Rinehart and Winston, 1965), pp. 28-44.

[5]Introduction to Theoretical Linguistics, p. 9.

[6]Quoted in Introduction to Theoretical Linguistics, pp. 15-16.

[7]Of course, if Chomsky's interpretation of the Port-Royal Grammar is correct (see below, pp. 40-41), its move to looking for this common structure elsewhere than in the surface features of the language was highly significant, and even revolutionary.

[8]Jakob Grimm was one of the Grimm brothers of "fairy-tale" fame. German romanticism of the period led to an interest in all sorts of "German antiquities" as representative of national character (thus rejecting the traditional classical excellence). Grimm dealt with two such "antiquities," old language and old stories. Incidentally, Grimm was not the first to formulate a version of "Grimm's Law." He worked on a foundation laid by a Dane, Rasmus K. Rast, in 1814, in Investigations Concerning the Origin of the Old Norse or Icelandic Language. A modern formulation of Grimm's Law, from Linguistics and English Grammar, p. 34, n. 6, is this:

Proto-Indo-European		Proto-Germanic
voiceless stops		voiceless fricatives
voiced stops	became	voiceless stops
aspirates		voiced fricatives

[9]A modern formulation of Verner's Law, adapted from
Linguistics and English Grammar, p. 34, n. 6, is this: "If
Proto-Indo-European voiceless stops are not initial or immediately following a stressed vowel, then Proto-Indo-European
voiceless stops become Proto-Germanic voiced fricatives."

[10]In English translation: Ferdinand de Saussure,
Course in General Linguistics, eds. Charles Bally and Albert Sechehaye in collaboration with Albert Riedlinger, trans.
Wade Baskin (New York: Philosophical Library, 1959; paper-
back, McGraw-Hill, 1966).

[11]Course in General Linguistics, p. 19. This is very
close to Chomsky's competence/performance distinction. See
below, p. 38.

[12]Course in General Linguistics, p. 126.

[13]Ibid., pp. 126, 130.

[14]This information is from R. H. Robbins, General
Linguistics: An Introductory Survey (London: Longmans,
Green, 1964), p. 78, n. for p. 48.

[15]Course in General Linguistics, p. 183.

[16]Edward Sapir, Language: An Introduction to the
Study of Speech (New York: Harcourt, Brace, 1921; paper-
back: Harvest Books, Harcourt, Brace, n.d.). I am using
the Harvest Books edition.

[17]Ibid., p. 25.

[18]Ibid., p. 60.

[19]Leonard Bloomfield, Language (New York: Holt,
Rinehart and Winston, 1933).

[20]Ibid., p. 161.

[21]Ibid., p. 22.

[22]Ibid., p. 27.

[23]Zellig S. Harris, Methods of Structural Linguistics
(Chicago: University of Chicago Press, 1951). It was actually written some years earlier; the preface is dated

January 1947.   It was reissued under the title Structural Linguistics (Chicago: Phoenix Books, University of Chicago
Press, 1960).   I am using the Phoenix edition.

[24]Ibid., p. 7, n. 4.

[25]Zellig S. Harris, "From Morpheme to Utterance,"
Language 22 (1946): 163.   For a more complicated description see Structural Linguistics, pp. 249-50.

[26]Zellig S. Harris, "Co-occurrence and Transformation
in Linguistic Structure," Language 33 (1957): 283-340.   Hereafter called "Co-occurrence."   In the same issue of Language
is Robert Lees's review of Chomsky's Syntactic Structures
(pp. 375-408).

[27]Zellig S. Harris, "Discourse Analysis," Language
28 (1952):   esp. 18-25.

[28]"Co-occurrence," pp. 285-86.

[29]Harris does not give a symbolism for this, but the
principle is clear enough.

[30]"Co-occurrence," p. 335.

[31]"Co-occurrence," p. 338.   A footnote to this sentence
(n. 67) adds: "This has been shown by Noam Chomsky...."

[32]John Lyons, Noam Chomsky (New York: Viking
Press, 1970), p. xii.

[33]Structural Linguistics, p. v.   This preface is dated
January 1947.

[34]"Co-occurrence," pp. 283-84, n. 1.

[35]Noam Chomsky, Syntactic Structures (The Hague:
Mouton, 1957), p. 6.

Chapter II

NOAM CHOMSKY'S REVOLUTION

Background

Noam Chomsky began the formal study of linguistics as an
undergraduate at the University of Pennsylvania, under Zellig
S. Harris. Harris suggested that the student Chomsky might
attempt a systematic structural study of some language, and
Chomsky chose modern Hebrew. The first version of this
study was an undergraduate thesis in 1949, and a more extensive version was Chomsky's master's thesis in 1951, Morphophonemics of Modern Hebrew. This study attempted to explain the distribution of phonetic forms in Hebrew and did not
develop its rudimentary syntactic component of grammar.
Chomsky reports[1] that he started the study by trying to apply
the segmentation and classification procedures of structural
linguistics, but soon reached a dead end. Not knowing what
to do next, he tried something that seemed more natural: he
constructed a system of rules for generating the phonetic
forms of sentences. In the process, he found it useful to
postulate abstract elements that could be mapped into phonetic
representation by general rules. Since this approach differed
so much from "real" linguistics, and since his work was
mostly ignored by the "real" linguists whom he respected,
Chomsky assumed for a long time that he was just indulging

in a private hobby.   However, he gradually became convinced that the methodological limitation of structuralism--the restriction to procedures based on substitution, matching, and similar "taxonomic" operations--was "arbitrary and unwarranted. "[2]   By 1953 Chomsky began writing what was finally published as The Logical Structure of Linguistic Theory, Chapter IX of which was essentially his Ph. D. dissertation. The first version was finished in 1955, and a partly edited and revised version was made early in 1956.   Copies of these were duplicated and circulated "underground" for twenty years, because Chomsky was not able to find a publisher for this extensive statement of what turned out to be the first of at least three stages in the development of his linguistic theory. It was eventually published in 1975, with only minor editing, and thus does not represent Chomsky's 1975 thought.   He allowed it to be published, apparently, for its historical interest as well as for the convenience of those who were citing the various mimeographed versions.

Chomsky reports that his manuscript was rejected by publishers "with the not unreasonable observation that an unknown author taking a rather unconventional approach should submit articles based on this material to professional journals before planning to publish such a comprehensive and detailed manuscript as a book."[3]   However, an article that Chomsky did submit to a linguistics journal was rejected, "virtually by return mail."   Eventually he did succeed in publishing articles in the proceedings of several conferences; one of these was "Three Models for the Description of Language."[4]   Finally, in 1957, Chomsky's notes for an undergraduate course he taught at MIT--an informal version of a small part of the material in LSLT and some additional material--was published as Syntactic Structures. [5]   For whatever reason (Chomsky credits a review by Robert Lees[6]), the book caught on, and within a few years many linguists were working on "transformational grammar."

The First Phase

This is often called the "Structures Phase," since the publication of Structures called attention to and popularized Chomsky's new method of doing linguistics.   However, the mimeographed versions of LSLT quickly began circulating, and they provoked the real discussions among linguists.   In LSLT Chomsky deals at some length with what the task of descriptive linguistics should be, and, of course, gives his suggestions for approaching and carrying out that task. Linguistic theory, he says, has two parts, syntax and semantics. Syntax is "the study of linguistic form"; it deals with what is grammatical. Semantics is concerned with "the meaning and reference of linguistic expression";[7] it describes "language in use," and is "an essential task for linguistics." Semantics and syntax are "parallel studies," with "many indisputable connections," although the boundaries between them are not at all clear.[8] These connections and correspondences "should be studied in some more general theory of language that will include a theory of linguistic form [syntax] and a theory of the use of language [semantics] as subparts."[9] However, important though semantics is, Chomsky himself proposes to study syntax only, and to study it in formal terms, independently of meaning. Since Chomsky was often misunderstood as saying that there was no interesting connection at all between linguistic structure and meaning, this is worth emphasizing.

Chomsky admits that it cannot be proved that the theory of linguistic form cannot depend on meaning. But he points out that there are many grammatical notions that do seem to have distributional, formal, grounds, yet none at all, at least so far, that has a semantic basis. Thus the question, "How can one carry out linguistic analysis without appealing to meaning?" loses its force when it is recognized that there is in fact no demonstrated alternative; no theory dependent upon meaning has, so far, been constructed.[10] There are, it is true, some instances in which it is claimed that linguistics relies on meaning. But some of the appeals to meaning, Chomsky says, are actually appeals to intuition, not meaning, and Chomsky himself proposes to appeal to intuition. Other claims to appeal to meaning are simply false. For example, it is often said that two utterances are phonemically distinct if and only if they differ in meaning. But homonyms--(river) bank and (savings) bank--and synonyms-- bachelor and unmarried man--falsify this statement in both directions. And, in fact, the method that a linguist actually uses to determine phonemic distinctness, the paired utterance test, does not rely on meaning at all. So it is at least reasonable to assume that a theory of linguistic structure is not based on semantic notions. Of course, if at any time it does not seem possible to give a certain notion distributional grounds, it can then be decided whether to admit a semantic base to grammar, or whether that particular notion is simply not part of grammar. But until then, says Chomsky, there is no point in "issuing manifestos";[11] we can only try to construct theories and test their adequacy.

Chomsky thinks that linguistics is concerned with three interrelated problems: first, constructing grammars for individual languages; second, developing an abstract, general theory of linguistic structure of which each individual grammar is an example; and third, justifying the grammars developed, showing that they are, in some sense, "correct." A grammar of a particular language is a scientific theory, and, like all scientific theories, tries to "relate observable events [observed utterances] by formulating general laws in terms of hypothetical constructs [phonemes, words, phrases, etc.], and providing a demonstration that certain observable events [other utterances] follow as consequences of these laws."[12] Note that, as in all scientific theories, only a finite amount of data (a corpus of utterances, in this case) is available for the formulation of rules, but that the rules, once formulated, "generate" other possible utterances.

The second problem, that of constructing a general linguistic theory, is obviously dependent upon the first, because if it were possible to construct complete grammars for all languages, it would be easy to abstract out a general theory. However, any attempt at an individual grammar must express itself in terms of some general linguistic theory. Similarly, if a powerful enough general linguistic theory were constructed, the grammars of particular languages would follow from it automatically. Thus the relationship between particular grammars and a general theory is circular, in the sense that each is dependent on the other, and a development in one will affect the other. However, a noncircular statement of the general theory and of a grammar as an example of it can always be made at any given moment in their development.

The weakest possible relationship between an abstract theory and a particular grammar is compatibility; obviously, as in the natural sciences, the elements of the grammar must agree with the requirements of the theory. However, linguists in fact have put stronger conditions on the relationship than those of any natural science. The strongest possibility, represented by the Bloomfieldian approach, is that a linguistic theory should provide what Chomsky called a "practical discovery procedure" for grammars--that is, given a corpus of utterances, a theory should provide a set of procedures enabling the linguist to construct mechanically the grammar of that language. This is much more than is expected of a scientific theory in any other area of science. Furthermore, Chomsky points out, linguistic theories that purport to give practical discovery procedures actually fail to do so.[13] A weaker possibility, also more than is expected of any other scientific procedure and also rejected by Chomsky, is that a theory should provide a "practical decision procedure" to determine whether a particular grammar (however it happened to be constructed) is the best possible one for a particular language. Chomsky suggests the adoption of what he calls a "practical evaluation procedure," which, although the weakest of the three named procedures, is still stronger than any requirement in the natural sciences. It says that a theory must provide a practical method of determining which of two proposed grammars (however constructed) is better. The qualifier "practical" is important; Chomsky feels that linguistic theory may be given in a strong enough form to provide a "literal discovery procedure" for grammars, although not a practical one, in at least some instances.[14]

To return to the third problem, that of justifying particular grammars, it is clear that every proposed grammar must meet whatever criteria of adequacy are internal to linguistic theory. Of course, the form of the grammar must be compatible with the form required by the general theory. But beyond that, Chomsky proposes that the evaluation procedure built into the general theory be that of "simplicity" of the resulting grammars. "Simplicity" is here the technical term from the philosophy of science, referring, roughly, to economy of means combined with power of results. Mathematicians often speak of it as "elegance."[15] "Simplicity" as applied to linguistic theory is analyzed by the philosophy of science, but "simplicity" of a grammar is a notion within linguistic theory, and can in principle be made precise. Chomsky tentatively takes "degree of generalization" to be the measure of simplicity of a grammar.[16] The choice of suitable notations to consolidate similar statements will be reflected in the length of a grammar, although of course reduction in length is not an end in itself. But appropriate systems of notation and conventions for their use (the "algebra" of the system) might enable linguists to evaluate certain aspects of simplicity in terms of length. Redundancies can also be eliminated by a hierarchy in the ordering of grammatical processes. But "simplicity" must be simplicity of the whole system; simplification on one level may lead to complication on another, and these must be weighed against each other. "If we can set up elements in such a way that very few rules need be given about their distribution, or that these rules are very similar to the rules for other elements, this fact certainly seems to be a valid support for the analysis in question."[17]

The form that a grammar may assume is thus crucial, and the form must be specified precisely. Chomsky
suggests that a great deal of economy can be achieved by
considering grammar to have a series of levels of representation, or "spellings," in terms of phonemes, morphemes,
words, etc. The representations are generated by "conversions," or rules of the form x→y ("rewrite x as y"). The
introduction of any particular level of representation--for
example, the morphophonemic level--may be justified by the
fact that one rule on this new level may replace several (or
even infinitely many) rules on another level. [18]

Besides meeting whatever internal conditions of adequacy a theory sets up, a grammar must meet certain external conditions or criteria of adequacy. The most important
of these is that the particular sentences generated by the
grammar must be acceptable to the native speaker, and that
the grammar must lead to analyses that are in agreement
with the intuition of the native speaker. Another external
criterion that Chomsky mentions is that the grammar must
explain satisfactorily cases of constructional homonymity, to
be discussed below, [19] but this explanation is something recognized by the native speaker's intuition. Chomsky seems a
little uneasy about this lapse from the structuralist ideal. He
calls these conditions "uncomfortably vague," and adds, "We
might hope that some more general account of the whole process of linguistic communication than we possess now may per-
mit us to reconstruct the criteria of adequacy for linguistic
theory in more convincing and acceptable terms. "[20]   But in
the meantime even a very small number of clear cases--that
is, weak conditions of adequacy for a given language--may
severely limit linguistic theory, since grammars for every
other language following from that linguistic theory must meet
the same external criteria of adequacy. Thus, while many
different grammars of the original language might meet the
original weak criteria, it is probable that very few of them
follow from a linguistic theory that produces suitable grammars of other languages. In this context the formulation of
the general theory provides a definition of "language. "[21]

Unsatisfactory as it may seem, the speaker's intuition
about linguistic form is the principal external criterion of
adequacy for Chomsky. Two misunderstandings are possible
here. First, linguistic theory is not based on intuition; intuition is not one of its primitive terms. The term does not
appear in the theory, but a native speaker's intuition judges
proposed grammars. A successful linguistic theory would be

a rational and systematic reconstruction of this intuition. Second, the appeal to intuition about linguistic form is not the same as an appeal to meaning. The now-famous sentence "Colorless green ideas sleep furiously" is intuitively grammatical but meaningless, while "Furiously sleep ideas green colorless" is intuitively both ungrammatical and meaningless.[22] Both sequences, by the way, had probably never occurred before Chomsky in English discourse and have an equal statistical probability of close to zero, and yet one seems grammatical and the other not. This is a counter-example to the attempt to measure adequacy by a high statistical order of approximation to English. Chomsky points out a parallel phenomenon on the phonemic level: "glip," for example, seems to be "grammatical nonsense," whereas "ligp" seems "ungrammatical nonsense."[23] One of the signs of the failure of previous linguistic theories, says Chomsky, is that if they are pushed beyond certain arbitrary (but intuitively significant) limits, their grammars are not only hopelessly complex, but counterintuitive.

Chomsky says that his own work at this time was not at all influenced by "information theory," which reigned nearly supreme in the late 1940s and throughout the 1950s in a great variety of disciplines.[24] Information theory was partly a result of efforts during World War II to break codes, and it was used in the development of machine languages. The general expectation was that further research would soon lead to machines able to speak and translate natural languages. As far as Chomsky was concerned this model of language had little plausibility and seemed to direct too much work toward problems that were of no interest or importance in themselves, that were "pointless as well as probably quite hopeless." But since "virtually every engineer or psychologist ... and many professional linguists as well, took for granted that the formal models of language proposed in the mathematical theory of communication provided the appropriate framework for general linguistic theory,"[25] Chomsky eventually had to deal with it. He considered the generative capacity of grammar based on this model, which he called "finite-state grammar" (FSG), in an appendix to Chapter VII of LSLT (when LSLT was finally published, however, that appendix was omitted). The material in that appendix was revised and published in the article "Three Models." The same three models are also discussed in Structures. Since FSG is the weakest of the three models, and since it was discussed first in Chomsky's earliest published material, and since it was a representative of what appeared to be the prevailing new theory at the time, the mistaken assumption was made that Chomsky's own work grew out of his interaction with this position.   However, that is not correct.   The central issue of LSLT was the comparison of what appeared in "Three Models" and Structures as the second and third models, what were eventually called "phrase-structure grammar" (PSG) and "transformational-generative grammar" (TGG).   FSG was mentioned only in that omitted appendix.

All three models of language use a finite set of symbols (the "alphabet" or vocabulary) to construct an infinite set of sentences by means of a finite set of recursive rules. A "string" is any concatenation of the symbols of the alphabet; those strings that are grammatical sequences are sentences.   A language is a finite or infinite set of sentences; in practice, the assumption is made that languages are infinite in order to simplify their description by allowing for recursive rules in the grammar.

The first model is that of a finite-state Markov process, or FSG.   FSG generates sentences from left to right. A sentence is produced by starting with the initial state (S_i), running through a sequence of connected states, each transition producing a word, and ending with the final state (S_f). Loops may allow repeating the same state or moving back to previous states.   As a simple example Chomsky provides this "state diagram,"[26] which contains this infinite set of English sentences: "The man comes," "The old man comes," "The old, old, man comes," ..., "The men come," "the old men come," "The old, old, men come," ..., etc.

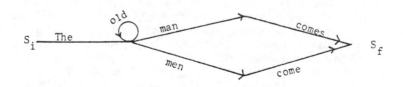

Here every element except the first is dependent on the element immediately preceding it.   Obviously the grammar quickly becomes very complex as larger subsets of English are considered.   But no matter how complex we are willing to allow it to become, English lies outside its range of description, as Chomsky proves rigorously in "Three Models" and somewhat less formally in Structures.   The gist of the proof is that there are subsets of English with dependencies between noncontiguous elements, which may be separated by other pairs of dependent noncontiguous elements. Chomsky gives these examples:[27] If S_1, S_2, S_3 ... are declarative sentences in English, then these are also English sentences:

If S_1, then S_2.
Either S_3 or S_4.
The man who said that S_5 is arriving today.

In each of these there is a dependence between noncontiguous words: if-then, either-or, man-is. Further, we can insert sentences with these dependencies into each other:

If either the man who said that S_5 is arriving today or S_4, then S_2.

(Chomsky suggests that this particular example will sound less odd if we replace "if" with, for example, "if it is the case that.") There are many possibilities in English for constructions of this sort, which seem to be clearly grammatical English sentences. But these sentences cannot be produced by an FSG, whose elements are dependent upon the immediately preceding element. Thus a fundamentally different sort of grammar is needed to generate English.

The second model of language Chomsky considers is phrase-structure grammar (PSG), a formalization and extension of Immediate Constituent Analysis. He works out an explicit theory of PSG, defining a system of levels of representation, each of which consists of elementary units (primes), an operation of concatenation that constructs strings, and relations defined on primes, strings, and sets of strings. Associated with each level is a level-marker of each sentence, which is the representation of that sentence on that level. LSLT considers the levels of phonetics, phonemics, word, syntactic category, morphemics, morphophonemics, and phrase structure--and, eventually, transformations. However, even before adding the level of transformations Chomsky has abandoned the taxonomic approach even at the lower levels by introducing abstract structures, such as level-markers. On the phrase-structure level phrase structure is determined by a finite vocabulary, a finite set of initial strings, and a finite set of "conversions" (phrase-structure rules or rewrite rules) of the form x→y. X need not be a single symbol, but only a single symbol of x may be rewritten in forming y. The initial strings (here only "Sentence")

do not appear on the right of any PS rule. In Structures
Chomsky gives the following simple example:[28]

PS rules:

    (1) Sentence → NP + VP
    (2) NP → T + N
    (3) VP → Verb + NP
    (4) T → the
    (5) N → man, ball, etc.
    (6) Verb → hit, took, etc.

With these rules we can construct this "derivation":

Sentence
NP + VP
T + N + VP
T + N + Verb + NP
the + N + Verb + NP
the + man + Verb + NP
the + man + hit + NP
the + man + hit + T + N
the + man + hit + the + N
the + man + hit + the + ball

We could construct other derivations--"equivalent derivations"
--for the same sentence by applying the rules in a different
order. All these equivalent derivations can be represented
by a "tree diagram" or "phrase marker," such as this:

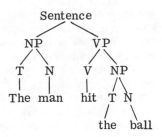

This simple example had rules with only one element on the
left; these rules are "context-free." The grammar of English can be greatly simplified if we allow "context-sensitive"
PS rules. For example, to deal with single and plural verbs
we might have such rules as this:

$$NP_{sing} + Verb \rightarrow NP_{sing} + hits$$

Still, only one element on the left is rewritten on the right.

Chomsky does not claim that English cannot be described in terms of a context-sensitive PSG, but he does claim that any PSG for English would be "extremely complex, ad hoc, and 'unrevealing.'"[29] For example, the system of English verb forms is full of interdependencies--"has taken," but not "has taking." This can be dealt with fairly simply, but only by using discontinuous elements in the rewrite rules, and by requiring reference to constituent structure (that is, to the history of the derivation). Another example is the active/passive relation. There are complicated restrictions as to when the element be͡en must be used and when it may not. The simpler solution, which eliminates duplications in the PS rules, would be to have a rule something like this:

If S_1 is a grammatical sentence of the form
NP_1 - Aux - V - NP_2,
then the corresponding string of the forms
NP_2 - Aux + be + en - V - by + NP_1
is also a grammatical sentence.[30]

Such a rule, which Chomsky proposes to call a "transformation," also lies outside the scope of PS grammar. Besides being simpler it has the advantage of appealing to the intuition of the speaker that, in some sense, an active sentence has a "corresponding" passive that, more or less, has the same meaning.

Chomsky's "transformations" were suggested by Zellig Harris's "transformations," but are quite different--so much so that Chomsky later said, "It probably would have been preferable to select a different terminology instead of adapting Harris's in this rather different context."[31] For Harris a transformation changes one sentence (say, an active) to another (say, a passive). A transformation in Chomsky's system works on an underlying string, not a sentence; all sentences are the result of transformations applied to the results of PS rules. The difference between a transformational rule and a PS rule is that a transformation converts a sentence with a given constituent structure into a new sentence with a derived constituent structure. It converts one phrase marker into another. To apply a PS rule one must know only the shape of the string to which it applies. To apply a transformational rule, one must know some of the history of the derivation of

the string to which it applies. Each particular transformation is associated with a "restricting class," and may apply
only to those strings that are analyzable in terms of that
restricting class. Chomsky formalized transformations by
giving the structural analysis (SA) of the strings to which a
transformation applies and the structural change (SC) it effects. For example, the (optional) passive transformation as
given in Structures:[32]

SA: NP - Aux - V - NP
SC: X_1 - X_2 - X_3 - X_4 → X_4 - X_2 + be + en - X_3 -
      by + X_1

In later works "structural analysis" is called "structural index" or "structural description."

Chomsky called this model of grammar "transformational grammar," but it is not purely transformational; it has
a P-S component also. And, like the other models, it has a
morphophonemic component as well. The transformational
component links the other two. Later, therefore, it was
named "transformational-generative" (T-G) grammar. In this
system there are two types of transformations: obligatory,
which must be applied--for example, transformations involving auxiliary verb forms--and optional, such as the passive.
Both the phrase-structure component and the transformational
component are ordered in terms of which rules apply in what
order. Applying only obligatory transformations gives kernel
sentences, a very small, probably finite, set of simple, active, positive, declarative sentences. All other sentences
("transforms") are derived from optional transformations on
the strings underlying these kernel sentences. The minimal
transformation-marker (T-marker) contains only the compound
transformation that maps phrase markers into strings of
words.

Chomsky sums up the whole process:

A grammar consists of a sequence of conversions
[rules of the form x→y] and a list of T-markers.
The conversions are divided into two parts, the
first leading from Sentence to terminal strings, the
second from strings of words to strings of phonemes.
We generate a sentence in the following manner:
    (1) Derive a terminal string from Sentence by
the first part of the sequence of conversions. From
this derivation, we can reconstruct uniquely the P-
marker of this string.

(2) Select a T-marker and apply it to the terminal string with the given phrase structure. If
the T-marker is just [the transformation which
maps a phrase marker into a string of words], we
have a kernel string; otherwise, a transform. In
either case, we have a string of words.
(3) Derive a string of phones from this string
of words by the remaining conversions. From this
derivation we can reconstruct the lower-level representations from the derived string.[33]

In diagram form it looks like this:

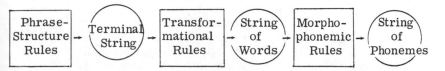

To go back for a moment to Phrase Structure grammar (PSG), it has the advantage over Finite-State grammar
of being "revealing"--of providing insight into the use and
understanding of language--for some sentences that display
the type of ambiguity that Chomsky called "constructional
homonymity." For example, the sentence "They are flying
planes" can be understood in two ways, represented by these
two phrase structure analyses (here simplified to make this
syntactical point only):

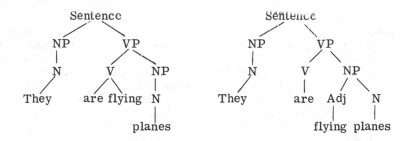

Some cases of constructional homonymity, however, cannot
be explained by PSG, but they can be explained by a transformational analysis. Chomsky's example is "the shooting
of the hunters." It has only one PS analysis, but it has two
possible transformational origins, corresponding to the two
kernel sentences "the hunters shoot" and "they shoot the

hunters." This is a case of transformational ambiguity, not PS ambiguity. Once the move to T-G grammar has been made, the first example, "They are flying planes," can also be explained as a case of transformational ambiguity, and Chomsky remarks, "It is not clear that there are any cases of constructional homonymity purely within the level of phrase structure once a transformational grammar is developed."[34]

The Standard Theory

Aspects of the Theory of Syntax, published in 1965, became the definitive expression of the so-called "Standard Theory."[35] In it Chomsky developed, changed, and in some places reinterpreted his earlier theory in the light of objections (some, he says, perfectly valid) and misunderstandings raised by it. He made two major changes: the first concerns the lexicon, and the second, transformations.

In the early theory Chomsky thought that the lexicon was inserted by conversions, or PS rules of the sort V→hit (actually, by a context-sensitive PS rule--add, "in the context NP_{plu}") to produce the final (terminal) string of a derivation. This is actually a purely structuralist slot-theory approach to the lexicon, because it assumes that lexical categorization is hierarchic in the same way that categorization of phrases is hierarchic. Chomsky credits G. H. Matthews with pointing out that this method is incorrect.[36] Lexical categorization typically involves cross-classification; nouns may be proper or common, animate or inanimate, human or nonhuman, for example, independently. Certain rules apply to the proper/common distinction; others to the animate/inanimate distinction; others to the human/nonhuman distinction. Chomsky observes that this problem of lexical cross-classification is formally identical to the problem of phonological cross-classification, in which, for example, some rules apply to the voiced/nonvoiced consonant distinction, or to the continuant/stop distinction, etc. So each phonological unit is assigned a set of binary features (e.g., +voiced), and phonological rules apply to segments containing specified features or groups of features. In a parallel way, each lexical item will have associated with it a set of binary syntactic features (e.g., +count, + animate, + human, + abstract), forming a "complex symbol."[37] The lexicon itself is an unordered set of lexical entries, each of which is a set of specified features, which may be phonological, semantic, and syntactic, but Chomsky limits himself to the syntactic.[38] Specific languages have "redundancy rules," which describe the inter-relations among various features.   For example, a phonol-ogical redundancy rule in English is that "in an initial se-quence # CC ..., if the second C is a true consonant (that is, not a liquid or a glide), the first must be [s]; if the sec-ond consonant is a liquid, the first must be an obstruent, etc."[39]   Similarly, there are syntactic redundancy rules to deal with the fact that when certain syntactic features are given, others are predictable.   Formulating these rules would make it possible to simplify lexical entries by removing re-dundancy features, leaving only idiosyncratic features in each entry.[40]   Chomsky further suggests that the rules generating complex symbols for N in a derivation are context free, but that those for V and Adj are context sensitive--sensitive to the complex symbols chosen for the nouns.   To choose the complex symbol for V independently and then to select N in terms of V leads to great complications.   It should be noted that in all this Chomsky considers himself to be dealing with the <u>syntactic</u> component of the grammar, not the semantic component.[41]

The second major change that Chomsky made con-cerned transformations.   Originally Chomsky had said that some transformations--e.g., the negative transformation--were optional; when used, they transformed what would other-wise have become a "kernel sentence" into a derived sentence, a "transform."   Such transformations affected the meaning of the sentence radically.   Several people questioned this. It. B. Lees challenged the formulation of the negative trans-formation, suggesting that the negative element was not in-troduced by a transformation but by the rewriting rules of the base.[42]   In a personal communication to Chomsky about the same time E. S. Klima raised a similar issue about the question transformation.[43]   These views were supported and elaborated, and the imperative transformation included, by J. J. Katz and P. Postal.[44]   As a result of all this Chomsky accepted the principle, applying it also to the passive trans-formation, that what he had called optional singulary trans-formations were really obligatory transformations dependent upon the presence of an abstract marker (e.g., NEG) in the string.   This means that in the standard theory, transforma-tions are meaning-preserving.   Chomsky is not here dealing with "stylistic" reorderings, which he regards as much less deeply embedded in the grammatical system.   In fact, they may be rules of performance, rather than of grammar (or competence).[45]

In the early theory the recursive element had been handled by "generalized transformations," which embedded a "constituent" clause into a "matrix" clause.[46] But investigation of embedding transformations seemed to show that they also did not introduce any meaning-bearing elements; they only interrelated the semantic interpretations of the phrase-markers involved. So an embedding transformation replaced a "dummy" symbol in the matrix clause. Finally, there appeared to be a linear ordering of singulary transformations, and they seemed to apply to constituent clauses only before embedding, and to matrix clauses only after embedding. These restrictions were pointed out by C. J. Fillmore,[47] and were not predicted by the theory.

So in Aspects Chomsky proposes eliminating generalized transformations altogether and provides for recursion by allowing the PS rules to introduce the initial category symbol (S); PS rules may therefore have the form A→ ... S ... (This was not allowed in the earlier theory). Thus the PS rules (which are linearly ordered) may apply cyclically, returning to the beginning of the sequence each time the PS rules introduce "S" again. This will result in a "generalized phrase marker," or "deep structure." Then the transformations, which are also linearly ordered, are applied cyclically, beginning with the most deeply embedded constituent sentence. What emerges from the transformations is called the "surface structure." The deep structure is the basis for semantic interpretation; the surface structure is the basis for phonological interpretation.

Chomsky summarizes the Aspects theory as follows:

> A grammar contains a syntactic component, a semantic component, and a phonological component. The latter two are purely interpretive; they play no part in the recursive generation of sentence structures. The syntactic component consists of a base and a transformational component. The base, in turn, consists of a categorial subcomponent [the phrase-structure rules] and a lexicon. The base generates deep structures. A deep structure enters the semantic component and receives a semantic interpretation; it is mapped by the transformational rules into a surface structure, which is then given a phonetic interpretation by the rules of the phonological component. Thus the grammar assigns semantic interpretations to signals, this association being

mediated by the recursive rules of the syntactic component. [48]

In diagram form the theory looks like this:

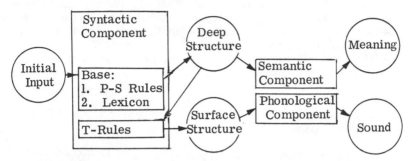

Chomsky has alternative descriptions of what constitutes the base, each of which had advantages and disadvantages. The first:

I.   Phrase-structure Rules
  A.   Branching rules (with no complex symbols; in practice, they seem to be context-free)
  B.   Subcategorization rules (with complex symbols)
      1.   Context-free rules
      2.   Context-sensitive rules ("really local transformational rules")
          a.   Strict subcategorization rules
          b.   Selectional rules

II.   Lexicon entries with binary features.
    This functions with a <u>context-free</u> rule governing insertion of lexical formatives. (The lexical rule need not be stated in the grammar because it is universal.)

The second description.

I.   PS rules: Branching rules, context-free

II.   Lexicon
  A.   Syntactic redundancy rules (Replacing B.1. in the first description)
  B.   Entries with binary features
      This functions with a <u>context-sensitive</u> lexical rule. [49]

Chomsky hypothesizes that the rules of the base (at least the context-free PS rules) may be universal, and that the category symbols appearing in them may form a fixed universal alphabet. The phonological features are drawn from a universal set of phonological features (the distinctive-feature system). Similarly, the semantic features are "presumably drawn from a universal alphabet," but little is known about this yet. [50] The particular choice and combination of features in the lexicon would be language-specific, as would the transformational rules. The transformational component acts as a filter; not everything that the base can possibly generate can be operated upon by the transformational component. Only those abstract structures that can be transformed into well-formed surface structures can be called "deep structures."

The distinction Chomsky made in his early period in terms of "corpus" and "language" he now makes in terms of "competence" and "performance." "Performance" is what a speaker (or hearer) actually does verbally in a concrete situation; obviously, performance is affected by all sorts of nonlinguistic factors--distraction, forgetfulness, illness, etc. "Competence" is the speaker's knowledge (not necessarily conscious) of his language. Then

> the problem of the linguist, as well as for the child learning the language, is to determine from the data of performance the underlying system of rules that has been mastered by the speaker-hearer and that he puts to use in actual performance.

This kind of idealization of grammar as competence is, Chomsky further argues, both necessary and legitimate. [51] Thus linguistics is really the study of mind, and is therefore a part of psychology. [52] Although this relation was not discussed explicitly in his early work, Chomsky claims that it was always part of the background of his thinking, but it was "too audacious" to mention. [53]

Chomsky claims that the human mind, in particular its language-learning faculty (which of course is not the only intellectual structure of the mind), is not a tabula rasa, on which any sort of language may be imposed. Rather the mind has a genetically determined structure that limits the possibilities for the grammar of a language. For example, the theory of grammatical transformations is structurally dependent; that is, transformations operate on strings that have been analyzed in terms of certain categories. A natural language (e.g., English) might have a question transformation that places Auxiliary Verb to the "left" of a preceding NP. But natural languages do not seem to have transformations that, say, reverse word order in any arbitrary string. There is no a priori reason why they should not; it appears to be an empirical fact that they do not.

Thus Chomsky hypothesizes that the investigation of these apparently innate structures of the human mind can lead to a "universal grammar," a description of the universal properties that determine the form of language. This is a set of conditions on grammar, not a core of rules for every grammar. To the extent that "universal grammar" can be determined, particular grammars can be simplified by eliminating from them all that is already described in universal grammar.

Chomsky sees as a historical forerunner of T-G grammar what he calls "Cartesian linguistics," that is, traditional linguistics of the seventeenth, eighteenth, and early nineteenth centuries, before linguistic theory rejected the idea of any innate mental faculties. As Chomsky interprets it, the Cartesians found that the theory of corporeal body, the prevailing explanatory model of the time, did not account for facts that were obvious. Descartes himself, who did not say much about language, did argue that the "only sure indication that another body possesses a human mind, that it is not a mere automaton, is its ability to use language in the normal way" where "the normal way" means creatively, expressing and understanding new thoughts. So the Cartesians invoked a "second substance, whose essence is thought, alongside of body."[54] Further, a great deal was made of the fact that human language seems to be species-specific, and qualitatively different from various systems of animal communication. Chomsky remarks that while the phenomena about language described by the Cartesians are real enough, their explanatory proposals of an active principle called "mind" were of no substance; however, he adds,

> Honesty forces us to admit that we are as far today as Descartes was three centuries ago from understanding just what enables a human to speak in a way that is innovative, free from stimulus control, and also appropriate and coherent.[55]

Nevertheless, he claims, this early linguistic theory, because it saw its task as "philosophic" or "universal" grammar, was very similar to post-Structuralist contemporary linguistics.

It is odd that Chomsky chooses the label "Cartesian" for this grammatical tradition, while rejecting Cartesian dualism so vehemently. He has received much criticism about the label. John Searle, for example, accuses him of making the historical claim that Descartes and others had a theory of language similar to his own. According to Searle, that is not true; Descartes thought that concepts were innate, but that language was arbitrary. Leibnitz is a more plausible historical antecedent. [56] Chomsky denies making that particular historical claim. He claims only that Descartes's appreciation of the creative use of language was like his own, and that he is following others, not Descartes, in the details of transformational grammar. The work that began the tradition was, in Chomsky's opinion, the Port-Royal grammar of 1660, Grammaire générale et raisonnée, by Claude Lancelot and A. Arnauld. [57] It developed its theory of language within a Cartesian philosophic framework. Robin Lakoff suggests that, although Descartes probably created a "favorable mental climate" for the ideas of the Port-Royal grammar, the true originator of this type of linguistics was a sixteenth-century Spaniard who taught at the University of Salamanca, named Sanctius. [58] Descartes is never credited by either Lancelot or Arnauld, but Sanctius is highly praised in the preface to the third edition (1654) of an earlier work by Lancelot, the Nouvelle méthode pour facilement et en peu temps comprendre la langue latine. (Chomsky rejects Sanctius's influence on insufficient grounds, according to R. Lakoff.)[59]

However, Chomsky's analysis of this grammatical tradition is more important than the label he attaches to it. [60] According to Chomsky, the Port-Royal grammar claims that language has two aspects, one the sound and the other the significance, or, the physical shape and how it expresses a thought. These need not be identical. There is a system of propositions (common to all languages) to which certain rules are applied to form sentences. These rules are different for each particular language. The system of propositions is not necessarily realized completely in the sentence produced. Chomsky sees this description as more or less what, in modern terms, would be deep structure mapped into surface structure by transformational rules. Furthermore, the Port-Royal grammar recognized these levels even though it was apparently the first grammar to use phrase-structure analysis systematically on the surface level.

Chomsky also wishes to include under the "Cartesian Linguistics" heading the general linguistics that developed during the Romantic period. (He does not claim that linguists of that period regarded themselves as being in the same tradition; in fact, he says they considered themselves to be reacting against Cartesian mechanism. He only claims that their most valuable contribution can be related to the Cartesian "philosophical grammar.") Wilhelm von Humboldt, for example, characterized language as "making infinite use of finite means." He also thought that language was inherent, at least to some extent, in the human mind and thus could not really be taught, but only elicited from the learner--perhaps by appropriate environmental stimuli. And he too sees a difference between "inner form" and "outer form" closely corresponding to "deep structure" and "surface structure."

One problem with these early attempts at generative grammar was that they did not have the technical recursive devices to cope with the creativity of language; such devices have begun to be developed only since the mid-1930s. Thus philosophical grammar reached its limits in terms of techniques that were then available, and linguistics naturally turned to comparative Indo-European and then the structuralist-descriptive approach, with the practical goal of trying to preserve something of the rapidly disappearing languages of primitive peoples. Then all the emphasis was placed on the surface structure, which seemed to show "the infinite diversity of human speech."[61] The conclusion was that "languages can differ without limit as to either extent or direction."[62] This seemed to discredit the very possibility of universal grammar. However, this approach restricted itself--with no a priori justification--to superficial aspects of language, while philosophical grammar claimed only that languages are similar at a deep, abstract level. Further, empirical investigation seems to show that, in fact, languages do not vary "infinitely" or "without limit"; they seem to have common restrictions, such as only structure-dependent transformations, that also have no a priori justification.

Chomsky's frequent appeal to "intuition" or "introspection" was often misunderstood. In his early work sentences generated by the speaker-hearer must be acceptable to the intuitions of the native, but there are hints that Chomsky would like to find a more "rigorous" criterion. In Aspects the intuitions are part of the data. Chomsky can define grammar as a "theory of linguistic intuition."[63] But the theory itself is not necessarily available to the user's intuition or introspection, any more than, say, a theory of vision is discoverable by intuition--although any such theory would of course have to agree with human experience.

Another misunderstanding arose from Chomsky's use of "mentalistic" and "rationalistic" to describe his theory of language. Chomsky distinguishes mentalism from, for example, dualism. The mentalist "need make no assumptions about the possible physiological basis for the mental reality that he studies. In particular, he need not deny that there is such a basis."[64] Chomsky himself thinks that there is in fact a physiological basis, as studies of innate structures of other kinds--vision and perception, for example--seem to provide at least a biological analogue to, if not exactly support of, an innate physical basis for language.

The Extended Standard Theory

In "Remarks on Nominalization"[65] Chomsky makes several suggestions for revising the Standard Theory. He suggests that, while certain nominals (gerundive nominals) may be transformations, other derived nominals may come not from transformations but from base rules involving optional complements. (This would be true for verbs and adjectives, too). If this is so, then "the base rules for any language will contain language-specific modifications of the general pattern."[66] He also suggests that all symbols, including the categorial symbols, could be regarded as sets of features, not just the lexical symbols. And in this article he introduces the double-shafted arrow ($\Rightarrow$) to designate transformations.

But the major difference between the Standard Theory and the Extended Standard Theory is that the EST allows surface structure to affect semantic interpretation. Chomsky had fairly early become convinced that some aspects of surface structure affected meaning; in a 1965 article, "The Formal Nature of Language," he already says that it is likely that surface structure plays some part in semantic interpretation.[67]

He says more about the matter in "Deep Structure, Surface Structure, and Semantic Interpretation."[68] In this article he discusses several things that made him alter the theory that only deep structure determined meaning. One feature of speech is the "intonation center" of an utterance, which receives the main stress and serves as the "point of minimal inflection of the pitch contour" (in English). Generally this intonation center is not represented in writing. Chomsky calls a phrase that contains the intonation center the "focus of information"; replacing the focus of information by a variable determines the "presupposition" of the sentence. For example, consider the question "Did the Red Sox beat the Yankees?"; under "normal intonation" Yankees is the intonation center and thus the focus of information; the presupposition is that the Red Sox beat someone. Thus a possible answer to the question (with this intonation) would be, "No, the Red Sox beat the Tigers." However, the question "Were the Yankees beaten by the Red Sox?" (again, "normal intonation") seems to have the same deep structure as the above active question, but the same answer is not possible, unless, of course, the presupposition is denied. Thus surface structure rather than deep structure seems to determine focus of information and presupposition, and each choice of focus and presupposition corresponds to one possible interpretation. [69] Chomsky points out that the "standard theory" can still be saved by setting up S→S' F P as the first rule of the grammar, where S' is the initial symbol of the categorial component of the base and F and P are arbitrary structures, functioning only in a later "filtering rule," which says that the generated structure is well formed only if F and P are identical with the surface-structure focus and presupposition. This, however, is only a "notational variant" of determining interpretation from surface structure and therefore redundant. [70]

Chomsky mentions a number of other cases in which surface structure seems to determine semantic interpretation and that led him to alter the standard theory. [71] For example, the surface structure position of elements even and only seems to contribute to the meaning of their sentences. The scope of negatives and quantifiers is determined by surface structure. Some properties of modals seem to need surface interpretive rules. And there are several other such examples. Chomsky concludes that the standard theory is false to the extent that at least some rules of semantic interpretation must involve surface structure features, in order to deal with these examples. However, the deep structure still determines the grammatical or thematic relationships that enter into surface interpretation, such as agent, goal, and instrument.

To deal with these and other problems Chomsky has recently developed a "trace theory of movement," in which every movement transformation leaves a "trace" in the original place of the moved element. This allows one to determine from surface structure just what the deep structure thematic relationships were. This theory is first developed in Chomsky's Reflections on Language and has been continued in more recent works.[72] The new deep structure is still what the transformations work on to produce the new surface structure (and, as before, the output of the base is called deep structure only when the surface structure is well formed). But new deep structure--which Chomsky to avoid confusion sometimes calls "initial phrase marker" or "D-structure"--is no longer the basis of semantic interpretation; the enriched surface structure--or "shallow structure" or "S-structure"--provides everything needed for at least those aspects of meaning that are determined by grammar. Interpretive rules, working on the new surface structure, produce representations in "logical form" (LF), whose syntax is not determined by formal logic, but is probably in fact "close to that of the standard forms of predicate calculus."[73] The representations of LF probably interact with other cognitive systems of the mind--for example, the one Chomsky loosely calls "common sense"[74]--to produce all the aspects of "meaning."[75] Other interpretive rules work on the same S-structure to produce the universal phonetic representations, or phonetic form, which become the sound. Although the details keep changing, a typical version of EST according to Chomsky's recent work would look like this:

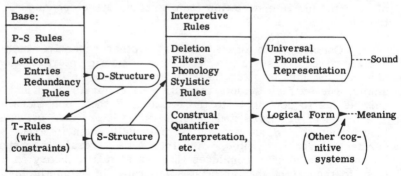

However, this is only a "typical" version, because several modifications are possible. In the introductory chapter of Essays Chomsky's description of EST accepts Joan Bresnan's suggestion that phonological rules apply within the cycle of transformations, and thus S-structure contains a phonetic representation.[76] In "Filters and Control" he does not follow that but remarks merely that if it is correct, "some modifications (though not essential ones)" would be required.[77] Similarly, it may be the case that the base generates only abstract features of the lexicon, and that the entries themselves are not inserted until the S-structure. In this case, also, the consequences would not be serious; "everything we say can be translated into an alternative theory."[78] There is also some terminological variation.

What Chomsky is trying to do in this recent work is to find ways to lessen the richness of transformational grammar, without sacrificing descriptive adequacy. He suggests that the way to do this is to specify conditions--as general as possible--on the various types of rules in the grammatical system. Insofar as this can be done, the number of rules of each type and the complexity of each rule can be lessened. Part of the motivation for this investigation is the process of language acquisition, or "growth," as Chomsky now calls it instead of the misleading "learning." The universal grammar a child possesses must somehow severely restrict the class of possible grammars the child can construct on the basis of limited experience--restrict it more than current universal grammar theories do--so that the evaluation processes can deal with the proposed particular grammars. Too many possibilities could not be evaluated.

Chomsky himself does not deal with constraints on the base rules; he refers his readers to the X-bar theory, which "takes the base to be in its essentials a projection from the lexical features [+Noun], [+Verb], by means of some general schemata."[79] Chomsky's work has concentrated on the transformational rules and on the interpretive rules that map S-structure into phonetic form and LF. He now claims that for at least a significant part of the grammar, which he calls "core grammar," there are only two principal transformational rules, NP-movement and wh-movement, both of which are cyclical and bounded and observe certain restraints.[80] He has even suggested that in fact there is basically only one transformation, α-movement, where α is an arbitrary phrase category, under suitable constraints.[81] Under this system some of the things that individual transformation rules used to do are covered by the general conditions on rules or moved to other parts of the grammatical system, to the base rules or to the interpretive rules. For example, the notion of surface filters, which are part of the interpretive rules that map S-structures onto phonetic representation, determine which S-structures are well formed; they thus cope with the removal of ordering, obligatoriness, and complex contextual dependencies

from the transformational system.   At the same time the filters account for some properties of complementizers.[82]   It
remains to be seen whether the extreme simplicity of the
transformational component is worth the complexity that may
have to be attributed to some or all of the other components.[83]

Chomsky's recent work has dealt with much more than
the details of T-G grammar.   Much of his post-Aspects writing concerns the importance of the study of language.   Its
greatest importance, he feels, is that understanding language
may lead to insight into human nature.   Chomsky rephrases
in current terminology the "Cartesian" position (which he
claims as an ancestor of his position) and says that it speculates that "rather sudden and dramatic mutations might have
led to qualities of intelligence that are, so far as we know,
unique to man, possession of language in the human sense
being the most distinctive index of these qualities."[84]   Universal grammar proposes to reflect properties of mind.   Thus
linguistics is a branch of psychology, since psychology is
"the field that seeks to determine the nature of human mental
capacities and to study how these capacities are put to work."
He adds immediately, "Many psychologists would reject a
characterization of their discipline in these terms, but this
rejection seems to me to indicate a serious inadequacy in
their conception of psychology, rather than a defect in the
formulation itself."[85]   The proposal that innate structures of
the mind determine language learning is not, Chomsky says,
in dispute; the controversy is over the nature of the innate
structures.   A typical "empiricist" view is that there are
certain general principles of learning, which are not species-
specific (humans, say) or domain-specific (language, say).
The innate structures need only be sufficient to account for
the applicability of this theory of learning.   Chomsky points
out that if this were true--if there were a general theory of
learning--then humans ought to be as superior to rats in,
say, maze-learning ability as they are in language-learning
ability.   But apparently rats and humans are roughly alike
in maze-learning ability; in fact, "white rats can even best
college students in this sort of learning."[86]   In Chomsky's
view the innate structure of the mind must be rich enough to
account for the speed with which a child learns a language
upon exposure to a very limited amount of data, some of
which must be disregarded as ungrammatical in various ways.
On the other hand, it must not be so rich as to exclude any
human language, since children do not seem predisposed to
learn any one particular language more than another.   So
Chomsky proposes that the child's properties of mind include

an innate schematism (the "universal grammar") and an evaluation procedure; the child then develops the grammar of the
language he is exposed to by using the evaluation procedure
to select among grammars compatible with universal grammar. The nature of the universal grammar and of the evaluation procedure, and the accuracy of the whole theory itself
are, Chomsky insists, dependent on empirical investigation.

The attraction of the so-called "empiricist" position,
Chomsky thinks, is due partly to a justified concern for empirical confirmation, which was lacking in earlier rationalist
work, and Chomsky's reformulations are, he thinks, put in
a way that is subject to empirical confirmation. But more
than that, empiricist ideology appeared to offer human freedom, in contrast to slavery to unchangeable human nature.
And it is perfectly true, says Chomsky, that oppressive
institutions have used some definitions of essential human
nature as justification for their oppression. In that light the
empiricist doctrine that human beings have no intrinsic nature,
but their "nature" is completely a matter of history, naturally seemed a great step forward. However, Chomsky
points out, empiricist doctrine can equally well be used to
justify an oppressive institution.

> If people are, in fact, malleable and plastic beings
> with no essential psychological nature, then why
> should they not be controlled and coerced by those
> who claim authority, special knowledge, and a
> unique insight into what is best for those less en-
> lightened?[87]

Chomsky claims that there is no contradiction between freedom and creativity on the one hand and a system of constraints and forms on the other. Lack of constraints produces randomness, not creativity. Language in particular

> is a process of free creation; its laws and princi-
> ples are fixed, but the manner in which the princi-
> ples of generation are used is free and infinitely
> varied.... The normal use of language and the
> acquisition of language depends on ... a system of
> generative processes that is rooted in the nature
> of the human mind and constrains but does not de-
> termine the free creations of normal intelligence,
> or, at a higher and more original level, of the
> great writer or thinker.[88]

So Chomsky claims that linguistic freedom is not hindered but made possible by such a system of constraints as he proposes. And further, with respect to human social and political freedom, he remarks that the study of human nature could lead to a social science "based on empirically well-founded propositions concerning human nature,"[89] and that such a social science could be a good foundation for social action.

In connection with these speculations of Chomsky, John R. Searle accuses Chomsky not only of misusing the terms "empiricist" and "rationalist" but also of saying that empiricist ideology facilitated racism, and that the effect of Chomsky's approach is to "smear the great empiricists with these veiled accusations of racism."[90]   In fact, Chomsky does not mention the great empiricists in this connection, and he explicitly says both that empiricism has been used to promote human freedom and that "Cartesianism" has been used to justify racism and oppression in general. Chomsky does say that empiricism was (as a matter of fact, not of necessity) used in combination with industrial capitalism to promote a racist ideology, and that, in his opinion, under present economic and social conditions, a theory of innateness, including innate creativity and freedom, is a better defense against racism than an empiricist or "tabula rasa" theory.[91]

For Chomsky, linguistics is a branch of psychology, but psychology is a branch of biology. In Aspects Chomsky contented himself with remarking that a rationalist "need not deny" a possible physiological basis for mental phenomena. He now claims that language is a "mental organ" that can be seen as analogous to other complex physical human organs. No one takes an "empiricist" view of physical development, that, for example, "the human organism learns through experience to have arms rather than wings, or that the basic structure of particular organs results from accidental experience. Rather it is taken for granted that the physical structure of the organism is genetically determined."[92]   This physical structure that is genetically determined includes developmental processes that may take years, or happen only at some particular stage in development, perhaps only with some particular environmental stimulus. Of course, the pattern may vary somewhat from individual to individual, but the scientist's interest is in the species pattern. Chomsky claims that speech is one human species-specific cognitive system, and that it can be studied in the same terms as, say, the system of human binocular vision. Recent studies seem to show that the visual system is built into the human brain, but "triggering experience" at a certain stage of the infant's development is necessary for the system to function properly. In the same way, knowledge of language "results from the interplay of initially given structures of mind, maturational processes, and interaction with the environment."[93] Some work on the neural basis for the binocular vision system has been done, and also for some other systems, and Chomsky is sure that for language also "specific neural structures and even gross organization not found in other primates (e.g., lateralization) play a fundamental role."[94] In any case all of this, he insists, is subject to empirical verification (or falsification); it is not a matter for unsupported assumptions, on the one side or the other, about what human beings must be like.

In these speculations Chomsky considers two other possible human cognitive systems, the one he calls (as a first approximation) "common sense"--the system of beliefs and expectations about the nature and behavior of objects--and another, confined to only a few human beings, called "knowledge of physics." "Common sense," like language, seems to be acquired fairly uniformly and fairly rapidly by everyone in a community, more or less independently of any special teaching. And, like grammar, it is only marginally, if at all, accessible to introspection. "Knowledge of physics," on the other hand, is far from universal among humans, requires slow and often laborious teaching/learning, and, when acquired, is conscious knowledge. Thus humans seem in some sense adapted to acquire language and "common sense," in a way that they are not adapted to acquire "knowledge of physics." Chomsky suggests that this adaption is genetic, analogous to human adaption to walking rather than to flying. He speculates that the human language faculty may possibly work only in conjunction with other innate mental faculties, such as "common sense." When we name something we assume certain commonsense things about the behavior of objects. As an example Chomsky cites Wittgenstein's "disappearing chair": if a chair kept disappearing and reappearing, we would be reluctant to apply the word "chair" to it.[95] "Common sense" can change, of course, independently of language; Chomsky says that pre-Newtonian common sense could not cope with the idea of an "occult" force capable of action at a distance, and that Newton himself tried to find a mechanical explanation for the cause of gravity. The mathematical success of the "new" physics led to the change of "common sense."[96]

Chomsky suggests that the particular genetic structure of the human brain might constrain the class of humanly accessible sciences. Some possible sciences might be outside the scope of admissible hypotheses for the human mind's "science-forming" capacity, just as some possible languages (e.g., structure-independent languages) are not accessible to human language-acquiring capacity. (And, one wonders, whether post-Einsteinian "common sense" is within the human "common-sense-forming capacity.") In particular, Chomsky thinks that the science of human behavior (including the use of language and everything involving the exercise of will) may be such an inaccessible science. "It might be that our inability to deal with this question reflects a temporary condition of ignorance, a defect that can be overcome, in principle, as science progresses." But on the other hand, "it is not excluded that human science-forming capacities simply do not extend to this domain ... so that for humans, these questions will always be shrouded in mystery."[97] That is of course only a suggestion and while plausible is far from demonstrated. In any case, it should not disturb anyone who thinks that such limitations of the human mind are the same structures that enable humans to construct cognitive systems in the first place, and that these constraints are a necessary condition for freedom and creativity.

Notes

[1]This history of the development of Chomsky's thought is from his 1973 introduction to his The Logical Structure of Linguistic Theory (New York and London: Plenum Press, 1975), especially pp. 25 ff. Hereafter, this work is referred to as LSLT.

[2]LSLT, p. 31.

[3]Ibid., p. 3.

[4]Published in I.R.E. Transactions on Information Theory, Vol. IT-2, No. 3, Proceedings of the Symposium on Information Theory held at MIT, September 1956. Hereafter called "Three Models."

[5]Syntactic Structures (The Hague and Paris: Mouton, 1957). Hereafter called Structures.

[6]Robert Lees, "Review of Noam Chomsky's Syntactic Structures," Language 33 (1957): 375-408. Reprinted in

On Noam Chomsky: Critical Essays, ed. Gilbert Harman
(Garden City, N.Y.:   Anchor Press/Doubleday, 1974), pp.
34-79.

[7]LSLT, p. 57.

[8]Ibid., p. 97.

[9]Structures, p. 102.

[10]LSLT, pp. 88, 93, 97.

[11]Ibid., p. 97.

[12]Ibid., p. 77.

[13]Structures, p. 52, n. 3.

[14]LSLT, pp. 85, 116.

[15]Chomsky refers the reader to Nelson Goodman, "On
the Simplicity of Ideas," Journal of Symbolic Logic 14 (1949),
228-29. LSLT, p. 114, n. 2.

[16]LSLT, p. 119.

[17]Ibid., p. 113.

[18]Chomsky gives some specific examples in LSLT, pp.
114-16.

[19]See above, pp. 33-34.

[20]LSLT, pp. 101-02. "If possible, with operational,
behavioral tests," he adds in Structures, p. 53.

[21]LSLT, p. 81.

[22]These sentences appear in LSLT, pp. 94-95 (and
elsewhere) and in Structures, p. 15. At this point it is perhaps appropriate to add "Coiled Alizarine," by John Hollander,
from The Night Mirror (New York: Atheneum, 1971), quoted
in On Noam Chomsky: Critical Essays, p. 1:

Coiled Alizarine

Curiously deep, the slumber of crimson thoughts:
    While breathless, in stodgy veridian,
Colorless green ideas sleep furiously.

[23]LSLT, p. 95, n. 18.

[24]Even in music theory amazingly enough; see Leonard Meyer, Emotion and Meaning in Music (Chicago: University of Chicago Press, 1956). Chomsky speaks of the place of information theory in the intellectual climate in Cambridge at the time in LSLT, pp. 39-40, and in Language and Mind, enl. ed. (New York: Harcourt Brace Jovanovich, 1972), pp. 2-3.

[25]LSLT, p. 40.

[26]Structures, p. 19.

[27]Ibid., p. 22.

[28]Ibid., pp. 26-27.

[29]Ibid., p. 34.   See also LSLT, p. 71.

[30]Ibid., p. 43.

[31]LSLT, p. 43.

[32]Structures, p. 112.

[33]LSLT, pp. 73-74.

[34]Structures, p. 87, n. 2.

[35]Noam Chomsky, Aspects of the Theory of Syntax (Cambridge, Mass.: MIT Press, 1965).   Hereafter, Aspects.

[36]Aspects, p. 79.

[37]Chomsky gives these examples but does not claim to be giving a full description of lexical features and their rela-. tionships, in Topics in the Theory of Generative Grammar (The Hague and Paris: Mouton, 1966), p. 70.   Hereafter called Topics.

[38]Aspects, p. 84; pp. 213-14, n. 15; Topics, p. 70.

[39]Aspects, p. 168.   Chomsky worked on the phonological component of English with Morris Halle.   See Chomsky and Halle, Sound Patterns in English (New York: Harper & Row, 1968).

[40]The redundancy rules may also relate one sort of feature to another--e.g., a syntactic feature to a semantic feature. Aspects, p. 214, n. 17.

[41]See below, pp. 71-75, for Fodor-Katz-Postal's discussion of the lexicon as part of semantic theory. Chomsky says,

> The interrelation of semantic and syntactic rules is by no means a settled issue, and ... there is quite a range of possibilities.... The approach I have adopted ... is a conservative compromise between the attempt to incorporate the semantic rules strictly within the syntactic component and the attempt to elaborate the semantic component so that it takes over the function of the selectional rules. Aspects, p. 159.

[42]Chomsky mentions these objections in Aspects, p. 132, and Topics, pp. 59-62. Robert Lees, The Grammar of English Nominalizations (The Hague: Mouton, 1960).

[43]Aspects, p. 132. See also E. S. Klima, "Negation in English," in The Structure of Language: Readings in the Philosophy of Language, ed. J. A. Fodor and J. J. Katz (Englewood Cliffs, N.J.: Prentice-Hall, 1964).

[44]Katz and Postal, An Integrated Theory of Linguistic Descriptions (Cambridge, Mass.: MIT Press, 1964).

[45]Aspects, p. 127. See above, p 38, for performance/competence.

[46]"Matrix sentence" and "constituent sentence" are Lees's terms, which Chomsky modified. Topics, p. 62, n. 2.

[47]C. J. Fillmore, "The Position of Embedding Transformations in a Grammar," Word 19 (1963): 208-31.

[48]Aspects, p. 141.

[49]The first description is assumed in Aspects Chap. 1, § 3, and Chap. 4, § 2. The second is assumed in Chap. 2, § 4.3 and in Chap. 3. However, Chomsky points out that, assuming the second, we end up having to state a condition that "is not statable directly in the form of a Boolean

structure index for a transformation. This fact, though of no great importance, might be taken as suggesting that the [first system] is preferable." Aspects, p. 156.

⁵⁰Aspects, pp. 141-42.

⁵¹Ibid., p. 4.

⁵²Ibid., p. 57; Language and Mind, p. 1.

⁵³LSLT, p. 35.

⁵⁴Language and Mind, pp. 6-7.

⁵⁵Ibid., pp. 12-13.

⁵⁶John Searle, "Chomsky's Revolution in Linguistics," The New York Review of Books, 1972. Reprinted in On Noam Chomsky: Critical Essays, p. 21. Searle also misunderstands Chomsky's "theoretical claim" to be that empiricists (and behaviorists in particular) do not admit the existence of any innate structures at all. In fact, the issue for Chomsky is the nature of the innate structures. See below, Chapter III, Section I. Searle does agree with Chomsky that the behaviorist stimulus-response model of innate structures is not adequate.

⁵⁷A recent English translation: Antoine Arnauld and Claude Lancelot, General and Rational Grammar: The Port-Royal Grammar, ed. and trans. Jacques Rieux, Bernard E. Rollin, with a preface by Arthur C. Dante and a critical essay by Norman Kretzmann (The Hague: Mouton, 1975).

⁵⁸Robin Lakoff, "Review of Grammaire générale et raisonnée," Language 45 (1969): 347.

⁵⁹Ibid., pp. 357, 359. For Chomsky's discussion of Sanctius, see Language and Mind, pp. 17-19.

⁶⁰What follows is Chomsky's analysis in his Cartesian Linguistics (New York and London: Harper & Row, 1966).

⁶¹Wm. Dwight Whitney, quoted in Language and Mind, p. 20.

⁶²In Martin Joos, ed., Readings in Linguistics, 4th ed. (Chicago: University of Chicago Press, 1966), p. 228. Quoted in Language and Mind, p. 77.

[63]Aspects, p. 19.

[64]Ibid., p. 193. He adds, in Language and Mind, p. 98:

> It is an interesting question whether the functioning and evolution of human mentality can be accommodated within the framework of physical explanation, as presently conceived, or whether there are new principles, now unknown, that must be invoked, perhaps principles that emerge only at higher levels of organization than can now be submitted to physical investigation. We can, however, be fairly sure that there will be a physical explanation for the phenomena in question, if they can be explained at all, for an uninteresting terminological reason, namely, that the concept of "physical explanation" will no doubt be extended to incorporate whatever is discovered in this domain, exactly as it was extended to accommodate gravitational and electromagnetic force, massless particles, and numerous other entities and processes that would have offended the common sense of earlier generations.

[65]In Readings in English Transformational Grammar, Roderick A. Jacobs and Peter S. Rosenbaum, eds. (Waltham, Mass.: Ginn, 1970). Reprinted in Studies on Semantics in Generative Grammar (The Hague: Mouton, 1972), pp. 11-61. Hereafter called Studies.

[66]Studies, p. 59.

[67]Language and Mind, p. 126.

[68]In Studies in General and Oriental Linguistics Presented to Shiro Hattori on the Occasion of His Sixtieth Birthday, Roman Jakobson and Shigeo Kawamoto, eds. (Tokyo: TEC, 1970). Reprinted in Studies, pp. 62-119, and in Semantics, pp. 183-216.

[69]Studies, p. 100. The examples are all Chomsky's.

[70]Ibid., pp. 101-02.

[71]Chomsky, Reflections on Language (New York: Random House, 1975).

[72]Chomsky, *Essays on Form and Interpretation* (New York: North-Holland, 1977), hereafter called *Essays*; Chomsky and Howard Lasnik, "Filters and Control," *Linguistic Inquiry* 8 (Summer 1977):   425-504; Chomsky, "Rules and Representations," the 1979 Kant Lectures, a series of four lectures given at Stanford University, 8-18 January 1979: now published as *Rules and Representations* (New York: Columbia University Press, 1980).

[73]"Filters and Control," p. 429.

[74]See above, pp. 49-50.

[75]*Essays*, p. 10.

[76]Ibid.   Joan Bresnan, "Sentence Stress and Syntactic Transformations," *Language* 47 (1971):   257-81.

[77]"Filters and Control," p. 428, n. 7.

[78]Ibid., p. 432, n. 18.

[79]*Essays*, p. 168.   In various places Chomsky gives some references for the X-bar theory: Joan Bresnan, "Transformations and Categories in Syntax," *Proceedings of the Fifth International Congress on Logic, Methodology, and Philosophy of Science*, University of Western Ontario, London, Ontario, 1975, R. Butts and J. Hintikka, eds., in press; J. Bresnan, "On the Form and Functioning of Transformations," *Linguistic Inquiry* 7:   3-40; N. Hornstein, "S and the $\bar{\text{X}}$ Convention," *Montreal Working Papers in Linguistics* 4:35-71; R. S. Jackendoff, *X Syntax: A Study of Phrase Structure*, *Linguistic Inquiry Monographs* 2 (Cambridge, Mass.:   MIT Press, forthcoming).

[80]*Essays*, pp. 205-06.   For my purposes it does not seem necessary to go into the details of the proposed conditions.   As an example, one such condition is "subjacency," which says that at any given stage of the transformational cycle, rules may apply to elements at that stage or the immediately preceding stage only.   *Essays*, p. 10.

[81]*Rules and Representations*, p. 145.   See also pp. 148, 153-56, 177-79.

[82]"Filters and Control," pp. 431, 433, 450.

[83]Emmon Bach, in "Comments on the Paper by Chomsky," Formal Syntax, Peter W. Culicover, Thomas Wasow, and Adrian Akmajian, eds. (New York: Academic Press, 1977), pp. 133-55, suggests that if this approach is developed, there will no longer be any need for transformations or deep structure in the system at all. See section 3.2, "What Cost Simplification?", pp. 139-40. The "Paper by Chomsky" in Bach's title is "On Wh-Movement," which immediately precedes Bach's article in the volume. One wonders also about the future of "move α" as the transformation in an inflected language like Latin, in which the syntactic importance of word order is minimal. The price of taking English as the point of departure may prove too high.

[84]"Language and Freedom," a 1970 lecture reprinted in Chomsky, For Reasons of State (New York: Vintage Books, 1973), p. 396. The footnote to the quoted sentence (p. 407, n. 6) adds: "I need hardly add that this is not the prevailing view."

[85]Language and Mind, p. 103.

[86]Norman L. Munn, The Evolution of the Human Mind (Boston: Houghton Mifflin, 1971), p. 118. Quoted in Reflections on Language, p. 19.

[87]Reflections on Language, p. 132.

[88]"Language and Freedom," p. 402. Actually this is Chomsky's description of W. von Humboldt's understanding, but it applies to Chomsky as well. Chomsky identifies himself with this aspect of von Humboldt's thought.

[89]Ibid., pp. 405-06.

[90]John R. Searle, "The Rules of the Language Game," Times Literary Supplement, London, 10 September 1976, § III.

[91]See Reflections on Language, pp. 128-32.

[92]Ibid., p. 9.

[93]Problems of Knowledge and Freedom (New York: Vintage Books, 1971), p. 23.

[94]Reflections on Language, pp. 40-41.

[95]Ludwig Wittgenstein, Philosophical Investigations, 3d ed., G. E. M. Anscombe, tr. (New York: Macmillan, 1953), p. 38. Cited in Reflections on Language, p. 46.

[96]Language and Mind, pp. 7-8. For a discussion of the relationship between language and how humans see the world--including "common sense"--see Benjamin Lee Whorf, Language, Thought, and Reality (Cambridge, Mass.: MIT Press, 1956).

[97]Reflections on Language, pp. 156 and 25.

Chapter III

CHOMSKY'S INTERACTION WITH ALTERNATIVE POSITIONS

Behaviorism: B. F. Skinner

"Behaviorism" is the name given to a group of related methods of thought in philosophy and psychology whose goal is to establish psychology as a science with methods as exact and results as predictable as those of the physical sciences. According to this point of view, past attempts to describe behavior, particularly human behavior, have used unobservable and unverifiable concepts, such as "intention," "volition," "idea," and "meaning." Since these are not objective entities they cannot be dealt with in a scientific way; therefore, they have only obscured the real issues and must be eliminated-- or at least redefined in terms of functional relations among observable events. Behaviorists tend to see behaviorism as a battle against, and the only alternative to, a kind of metaphysical dualism that posits a quasi-objective existence to these imaginary mental entities. For behaviorists all events can, in theory, be analyzed in terms of cause and controlled by scientific methods, whether the events are human actions, such as language, or animal behavior, or happenings on the atomic level. There is no qualitative difference, for example, between the behavior of a laboratory rat pressing a bar when a light flashes to get a food pellet, and a human being saying something; both can be explained in terms of stimulus and response. A quantitative difference is usually admitted; human behavior is more complex. Some behaviorists are convinced that research and experimentation will eventually succeed in overcoming the complexity and provide means to analyze, predict, and possibly control human behavior. Others believe that the complexity of human behavior is such that no practical prediction or control procedures will ever be devised. In the field of language Leonard Bloomfield, who was a behaviorist, was convinced that, in theory, all speech could be explained as response to complex stimuli. In practice, however, it would not be possible for anyone to obtain all the data necessary for such an explanation.

B. F. Skinner is much more optimistic about the possibility of a behaviorist interpretation of language.[1] In his opinion recent experimental work has led to real progress in the analysis of behavior, and, although most of this experimental work has been done on animals other than human beings, it has been shown that the results are on the whole applicable to human behavior.[2] His claim is strong: "... the basic processes and relations which give verbal behavior its special characteristics are now fairly well understood."[3] Therefore, scientists will probably be able to find, gradually, "causes" of verbal behavior along the lines of the "causes" in the other natural sciences; it is now possible to begin to produce a "causal" analysis of verbal behavior whose success can be measured by "the extent to which we can predict the occurrence of specific instances and, eventually, [by] the extent to which we can produce or control such behavior by altering the conditions under which it occurs."[4] Skinner identifies the weakness of prebehaviorist attempts to explain language as the readiness to substitute "fictional causes"--ideas, images, meanings, or other events that take place inside the organism and that cannot be independently observed--for real, observable causes. Of course, this practice hampered the study of language, just because it is "the function of an explanatory fiction to allay curiosity and to bring inquiry to an end."[5] Skinner himself intends to analyze verbal behavior without using any such hypothetical entities. The facts of verbal behavior are plentiful, easily accessible, and thus well known; no particular experimental support for them is necessary. Skinner does occasionally cite the results of experimental work, for example, psychological word-association tests, but most of his examples are literary or conversational. He proposes to organize and arrange this data in accordance with the analysis of behavior, which comes from

careful experimentation, without assuming anything unique
about verbal behavior. Thus verbal behavior is a subdivision
of human behavior, which in turn is a subdivision of behavior
in general.

Skinner chooses the locution "verbal behavior" because
he wants a term that will not be confused with any traditionally used term, that will include more than just vocal behavior, that will point to the behavior of the individual speaker
rather than to that of a linguistic community, and that will
still cover what has traditionally been covered by language
studies. As a first definition, verbal behavior is "behavior
reinforced through the mediation of other persons,"[6] as distinguished from behavior that acts upon the environment directly through mechanical action. Thus verbal behavior includes not only vocal behavior and written behavior, but sign
and touch languages as well as all other forms of what might
be called signaling behavior: hand clapping, bugle blowing,
telegraphing, pointing, ceremonial manipulation of physical
objects.[7] The definition is later refined by specifying that
the other persons' responses must be conditioned responses,
and "conditioned precisely in order to reinforce the behavior
of the speaker."[8] This is meant to eliminate as "verbal" the
behavior, for example, of a prizefighter or a surgeon, who
achieve their results through the "mediation of other persons."
Vocal behavior is the most common and easily available sort
of verbal behavior, so Skinner deals primarily with it, but
he uses examples of other types, particularly literary.

Skinner intends to apply to verbal behavior the principal tools developed in experiments with animal behavior: the
three notions of stimulus, response, and reinforcement. In
the laboratory a stimulus is some part of the environment,
and a response (or operant) is a part of an animal's behavior, if a connection between the two can be experimentally
demonstrated and shown to behave according to dynamic laws.
A stimulus that produces a change in the strength of a re-
sponse--i. e., one that increases the probability that that response will be emitted--is a reinforcement. In these experiments gradual changes in the conditions of reinforcement can
lead to responses of some complexity; for example, a pigeon
can be conditioned to walk in a figure-eight pattern by a process of "progressive approximation" or "differential reinforcement." At first, any slight movement is reinforced. As
the pigeon "learns," reinforcement is successively held back,
until more and more of the desired response is emitted.
Eventually the pigeon makes the entire pattern before

reinforcement. Reinforcement is also necessary to maintain
a response; a response that is never reinforced gradually
becomes extinct. Skinner states the relation of the three
notions thus: "In the presence of a given stimulus, a given
response is characteristically followed by a given reinforcement."[9] The predictable correlation is between the response
and the reinforcement, but a relation between the response
and a prior stimulus is "the almost universal rule."[10]

Skinner then proceeds to analyze verbal behavior in
these terms. Language acquisition in a child, for example,
is exactly like a pigeon learning to walk a figure-eight pattern, except that the process is more complex. But it is
the same method of progressive approximation. At first any
approximation to even a small part of an appropriate verbal
response is rewarded or reinforced. Then little by little
reinforcement is gradually withheld until more and more of
the desired behavior is emitted. In this way the child eventually learns the verbal behavior considered appropriate in
the verbal community.

Skinner also attempts to analyze types of verbal behavior, inventing new terminology so as not to beg any question or cause any confusion with earlier "mentalistic" notions.
He considers, among others, "mands," responses to verbal
stimuli, "tacts," and "autoclitics." A "mand" is a type of
verbal response that, in a given verbal community, is usually
followed and reinforced by some particular consequence. Here
there is no need to appeal to the intention of the speaker,
only to the probable behavior of the listener. (Skinner adds
that, in general, intention can be reduced to "contingencies
of reinforcement."[11]) A command, for example, is really a
mand in which the listener's behavior is reinforced by reduc-
ing or eliminating a threat; a prayer is a mand that "promotes
reinforcement by generating an emotional disposition"; a request is a mand in which "the listener is independently moti-
vated to reinforce the speaker."[12] Skinner admits that people behave verbally in mand-like ways even when it is not
reasonable to expect reinforcement, for example, by manding
babies or dolls. These are "extended mands," merely exten-
sions of the same process. There are many other deviant
subtypes: "superstitious mands," "magical mands," and
mands in literature, particularly in lyric poetry.

Another type of verbal behavior is that which is a response to verbal stimuli. The simplest is "echoic behavior,"
in which the response is identical to the stimulus. The most

important other subtype is called "intraverbal behavior," in which the response is different from the stimulus, as in word associations, or the response "four" to the stimulus "two plus two." Verbal behavior that involves nonverbal stimuli is called a "tact." The two most important stimuli for tacts are the audience and the physical environment. A tact is a verbal operant "evoked (or at least strengthened) by a particular object or event or property of an object or event."[13] Here too Skinner must immediately move to the "extended tact"--one in which there is no one-to-one correspondence between the stimulus and the tact. However, the tact is a very important verbal operant because of the possibilities of controlling the stimulus. In practice it may be difficult to isolate the properties of the stimuli that are relevant; an example is the attempt to name the composer of a piece of music being played. But the theory of meaning becomes very simple: to discover meaning, "manipulate stimuli and, through the presence or absence of the response, identify the effective controlling properties."[14] This is difficult in practice not only because so many of the stimuli are trivial, incidental, and fleeting, but also because many of them are private to the speaker and thus unobservable--for example, the stimulus that leads to the response "My tooth aches." Further, "self-tacts" are behavior controlled by the "behavior of the speaker, past, present, or future."[15] Thus "I am looking for my glasses" is approximately the same as "When I have behaved this way in the past, I have found my glasses and have then stopped behaving in this way."[16] The necessity for such heavy reliance on private stimuli is uncomfortable for Skinner, who admits that unobservable behavior leads to "embarrassing gaps in our account." But he concludes that such covert behavior can be explained by the same procedures as overt behavior.[17]

The situation is further complicated by the fact of multiple causation: "... the strength of a single response [the probability that it will occur] may be, and usually is, a function of more than one variable and a single variable usually affects more than one response."[18] This does not mean, Skinner insists, that behavior in a specific situation is not fully determined; it only means that all variables must be considered in predicting or controlling behavior. The speaker is not an "inner agent" with intention, meaning, etc., but the locus of a complexity of variables, possibly even a unique combination of variables, which produces a possibly unique verbal response.

Thus a person's verbal behavior can be modified by modification of the controlling variables, and one way to do that is to do it verbally. To such verbal behavior, intended to modify the listener's reaction to behavior it accompanies, Skinner gives the name "autoclitic."[19] Of course, a speaker can be his own listener, and if this behavior is covert or not observable, for whatever reason--perhaps to avoid punishment or just to save labor--it is called "thinking." (There may be small-scale, theoretically observable physiological movements involved, but they do not have to be identified to deal with thinking scientifically.) Autoclitics are of many subtypes, for example, descriptive autoclitics, such as "I see" and "I tell you," and qualifying autoclitics, such as negatives. The category of autoclitics also includes grammatical processes in general. In Skinner's opinion the "raw responses" are roughly what were traditionally called nouns, verbs, and adjectives; "putting in the grammar" is a relatively arbitrary autoclitic process, which sets forth the order and relation involving the raw responses.[20]

In the course of the development of his work Skinner quotes, among others, Sheridan, Keats, Joyce, Ogden Nash, Sinclair Lewis, Shakespeare, Thoreau, Dickens, Gertrude Stein, and the Rev. W. A. Spooner. But he comes to the conclusion that, since interpretation is enabling the listener to infer plausibly what the stimuli could have been for the verbal behavior in question, it is therefore almost impossible in most cases of literature. The literary material is usually not a simple response but is often rewritten again and again, removing, for example, some of the responses that were themselves stimuli for other responses that remain. Furthermore, where such an intraverbal relationship between a stimulus and a response remains in the literary material as it comes to us, the order in which they evoked each other--that is, which was stimulus and which response--is almost always lost. Thus the ultimate listener cannot duplicate the author's determining conditions, and Skinner concludes, "In short, we lack the information needed for anything but the most superficial interpretation."[21]

Skinner concludes Verbal Behavior with a postscript describing a challenge that led him to investigate verbal behavior. He describes being seated at a dinner in 1934 next to A. N. Whitehead and explaining behaviorism to Whitehead, apparently with all the zeal of an evangelist. Whitehead listened carefully and courteously, then suggested that even if behaviorism should accomplish all that Skinner was claiming for it, human language would remain outside its scope. Whitehead ended with this challenge: Skinner was to explain, in behaviorist terms, why Whitehead uttered at that moment the sentence "No black scorpion is falling upon this table."

Skinner points out that it would be impossible for a physicist now to explain why the temperature in that dining room fluctuated that night, because the necessary data has been lost; the most a physicist can do is offer plausible causes, such as that someone opened a window. Similarly, the data that could identify the causes of Whitehead's sentence are no longer available, but Skinner is now ready to offer a plausible cause: Whitehead's "black scorpion" was a metaphorical response to the topic under discussion--behaviorism![22]

Chomsky responded to Verbal Behavior in a review that came out two years later.[23] He remarks that for anyone studying the causes of behavior, the only data is the observable input to the organism and the observable output of the organism; the problem is finding how the two are related. In insisting on this Skinner has done nothing new or remarkable. What is unusual is Skinner's claim that the only important inputs and outputs are of the sort that can be described as stimuli, responses, and reinforcements in the technical terminology of the laboratory, and that the relation of the input to the output is the very simple one of stimulus-response. The organism that "connects" the input and the output makes no important contribution to the process. In language the speaker's contribution to verbal behavior is no more than or different from (except perhaps in complexity) the rat's contribution to bar pressing, and therefore the methods of study successful with laboratory animals do not have to be significantly modified to apply to human behavior. Chomsky says that even most behaviorists do not share Skinner's opinion that "real progress" has been made in animal behavior or that the results are so easily applied to human behavior.[24] But leaving that aside, and also putting aside for the moment the intrinsically unlikely assumption about the irrelevance of the structure of the organism, Chomsky proceeds to examine Skinner's claim that verbal behavior can be precisely accounted for in strictly behaviorist terms. Chomsky shows that each time Skinner moves a technical term out of the laboratory, where it has a precise meaning, and applies it to verbal behavior, the term loses its objectivity and becomes a metaphor. If such a term is used with its scientific meaning, it applies to only a very limited area. For example, if

Skinner's definitions are taken seriously, very little of his book is about "verbal behavior."[25] Furthermore, when the terms are used metaphorically, they are no improvement over traditional terms, such as "meaning" or "reference"; they tend to obscure possibly useful distinctions that the traditional terms preserve.

In the first place, there are serious problems with Skinner's definition of verbal behavior. Even Skinner's extended definition[26] would include, among other things, rats pressing a bar and children brushing their teeth, assuming that the reinforcing behavior of the psychologist and the parent is conditioned. On the other hand, a warning "Watch out for the car" followed by a pedestrian's jumping to safety would not be verbal behavior, unless the pedestrian had been conditioned to jump in order to reinforce the speaker.[27]

There are also problems with Skinner's three major technical terms: stimulus, response, and reinforcement. In the laboratory a stimulus is an observable part of the environment and a response is an observable part of behavior; the two are related according to a smooth and reproducible function. But all this objectivity is lost when the terms are applied to verbal behavior. Skinner says that the stimulus is still part of the environment, some property or combination of properties of physical objects. But in fact the stimulus usually cannot be identified until the response is emitted. This makes the whole notion of stimulus empty, since it is only what the response says it is. And of course Skinner's claims of control of verbal behavior are equally empty, since it is impossible to control exactly which property a speaker will respond to. Chomsky points out several of Skinner's examples in which the so-called controlling stimulus admittedly "need not even impinge upon the responding organism"; for example, Skinner says that the statement "This is war" may have as stimulus a "confusing international situation." Chomsky concludes that "controlling stimulus," as Skinner actually uses it, is equivalent to traditional "denote" or "refer." Similarly, "response [strength]" is defined as "probability of emission," but probability is used as a cover for "interest," "intention," "belief," etc.[28]

"Reinforcement," the third major notion borrowed from animal experiments, also loses its scientific meaning; it need not even be the effect of an identifiable stimulus. Automatic self-reinforcement occurs when one talks to oneself, and an artist or writer is reinforced by the effects his works have

on others, "although he may not be reinforced often or immediately"--or even, presumably, until long after he is dead.
Thus "reinforcement" adds nothing to traditional descriptions
of wanting, wishing, liking, etc.; it is used as a cover term
for anything that has to do with motives for acquiring and re-
taining language.[29]

Chomsky also discusses some of Skinner's own classifications: mands, verbal responses to verbal stimuli, tacts,
and autoclitics. As in the case of "stimulus," there is no
way to identify the controlling variables, except from the fact
that the speaker has said what he or she said. However, even
if this problem could be overcome the definition of a mand
suffers from the fact that most people are not in a position
that their mands are usually reinforced. With regard to responses to verbal stimuli, Chomsky shows that Skinner's account of echoic behavior is simply false, particularly his assertion that the range and precision of echoic behavior is
completely determined by how strict the verbal community's
standards of reinforcement are. For example, Skinner does
not explain how a child's high voice "echoes" a father's bass
stimulus. Nor does he explain how children pick up a second
language or local dialect from other children--a verbal community not noted for the practice of "successive approximation" in Skinner's sense. Nor does he explain how children
learn correctly very precise sound distinctions that the verbal
community supposedly reinforcing them is usually completely
unconscious of--for example, the careful distinctions in English between aspirated and unaspirated "t" or "p" in certain
positions. The notion of intraverbal response no doubt has a
certain limited validity, but Skinner extends it to cover,
among other things, educated guesses, translations and paraphrases, and all the facts of history and science. The sort
of training that might cause a person to respond "four" to
"two plus two" cannot possibly explain the "large segments of
scientific, mathematical, and literary discourse" that Skinner
claims for it.[30]

Skinner's tacts suffer from the confusion about stimulus
already discussed, since a tact is defined as a response to a
nonverbal stimulus. But since the stimulus must be current,
any verbal behavior involving past, future, or possibility must
be a response to a current private set of stimuli, events oc-
curring within the speaker at the time of speaking. Most
tacts in real life, therefore, are responses to private stimuli, and again not to identifiable external stimuli.

Finally, Chomsky shows the inadequacy of Skinner's category of autoclitics. In one example Skinner suggests that, in the sentence "All swans are white, " "all" is an autoclitic modifying "Swans are white" and is equivalent to "always" or "always it is possible to say. "[31] Chomsky points out that, in the first place, the "reduced" sentence "Swans are white" is just as difficult to account for in Skinner's system as the original sentence. And Skinner's suggested equivalent cannot possibly be taken literally; it is false in both directions. It is possible to say any number of other things, or it might, for some reason, not be possible to say anything at all. As for Skinner's suggestion that grammatical processes are autoclitics, Chomsky says that the idea of "lexical items in a grammatical frame" is not at all new; Skinner adds only the "very implausible speculation" that nouns, verbs, and adjectives come first and are then related by autoclitic responses.[32] Thus here also Skinner has added nothing particularly new and original.[33]

To sum up this part of Chomsky's argument: he has shown in detail that Skinner's claim to scientific precision is simply false; that Skinner's technical terms are not applicable to human linguistic use when taken literally, that is, in their laboratory sense; and that when taken metaphorically, as Skinner actually uses them, they are no improvement over more traditional terms, but rather obscure distinctions important in traditional accounts.

Chomsky also attacks Skinner's initial assumption that external factors are most important with respect to human language behavior and that the structure of the human organism makes no special (much less unique) contribution to the process. Skinner does not offer experimental data to support this assumption. He does claim that language is acquired by progressive approximation. Presumably he considers this supported by the facts he calls "well known to every educated person and [which] do not need to be substantiated statistically or experimentally at the level of rigor here attempted. "[34] It is quite probable that many educated people do share Skinner's assumption about language learning, perhaps in a milder form, and do take time and trouble to "drill" their children as they begin to speak. But the assumption is not true; children in fact learn much more than they are specifically taught, about pronunciation as well as about grammatical processes.[35] And the ability of both children and adults to produce and recognize new and different sentences is not explained by calling the sentences "similar" to ones already reinforced, because the sense in which they are "similar" is never identified.

Even with respect to animal learning, reinforcement does not seem universally necessary for learning, at least when reinforcement is taken in its technical, not metaphorical, sense. There seem to be many examples of animals learning as a result of "idle curiosity" and similar "unmotivated" behavior. And there is the phenomenon of "imprinting," or an animal's exposure to objects or patterns at some critical stage in its life. This exposure results in perhaps very complex behavior patterns later, often emerging only after other stages in the animal's development. The maturation of the animal and its nervous system also seems to be a factor in the development of complex patterns of behavior. In effect, Chomsky is arguing not that Skinner is too scientific, but that he is not scientific enough; he has not taken into account a large amount of recent scientific investigation. A much more plausible hypothesis, in the light of currently available evidence, would recognize that

> reinforcement, casual observation, and natural inquisitiveness (coupled with a strong tendency to imitate) are important factors, as is the remarkable capacity of the child to generate, hypothesize, and "process information" in a variety of very special and apparently highly complex ways which we cannot yet describe or begin to understand, and which may be largely innate, or may develop through some sort of learning or through maturation of the nervous system.[36]

Chomsky suggests that much more research is needed before the relative importance of all these factors--innate structure, maturation, and experience--can be established. In particular, before we can understand what causes verbal behavior, or how the behavior is acquired, we need to understand better the nature of the behavior. (This is the distinction that he later calls performance/competence.) The particular task that is a reasonable and possible one for linguistics now is the characterization of the competence: that is, the development of grammars for particular languages and of a general theory of language. If this were accomplished, the discussions of meaning and causation of behavior might be more profitable. Chomsky seems to suggest that the laboratory data Skinner has collected--for example, the results of psychological word tests--may be perfectly valid as far as they go, but

they belong under performance, and the study of performance
--or verbal behavior--is hopelessly premature.

Skinner is quite right that the verbal behavior of speaker, listener, and learner is the only accessible data. But
the data seem to include such facts as that

> a child is capable of constructing an extremely com-
> plex mechanism for generating a set of sentences,
> some of which he has heard, [and] that an adult can
> instantaneously determine whether (and if so, how)
> a particular item is generated by this mechanism,
> which has many of the properties of an abstract de-
> ductive theory.... If this is correct, we can pre-
> dict that a direct attempt to account for the actual
> behavior of speaker, listener, and learner, not
> based on an a priori understanding of the structure
> of grammars, will achieve very limited success.[37]

Skinner's assumption that the contribution of the speaker was
minimal, almost nonexistent, led--contrary to his intention--
to a "mentalistic" theory in which some traditionally important distinctions were lost. Chomsky hopes to retain the insights of traditional theories but remove their obscurities and
put language theory on a scientific basis without any reduc-
tionism. It is of interest that both Chomsky and Skinner consider linguistics to be a branch of psychology; the difference
is that Skinner calls psychology the study of behavior, but
Chomsky calls it the study of the mind.

Semantics: The Shift Toward "Meaning"

One assumption about linguistics that Chomsky shares
with structuralists and that he defends with some vigor is the
independence of syntax from other parts of language, and
particularly from meaning. He has never denied that meaning
is related to syntax in probably interesting ways. But in his
early period he did not consider meaning to be part of linguistic description at all; he discussed only syntax and left
semantics for later, while admitting that the boundaries between them are far from clear.

In Aspects Chomsky takes semantics to be part of linguistic description and investigates the boundaries between
syntax and semantics at various points, trying to discover
the consequences of taking one position or the other on

several issues. Perhaps not surprisingly, he puts almost everything he investigates into the syntactic component--and yet allows for a semantic component also as part of the grammar. He calls his results "a conservative compromise between the attempt to incorporate the semantic rules strictly within the syntactic component and the attempt to elaborate the semantic component so that it takes over the function of the selectional rules."[38] However, he does not claim that he has settled anything; he sums up his whole discussion of the boundary between syntax and semantics with the comment:

> To conclude this highly inconclusive discussion, I shall simply point out that the syntactic and semantic structure of natural language evidently offers many mysteries, both of fact and of principle, and that any attempt to delimit the boundaries of these domains must certainly be quite tentative.[39]

That Chomsky includes a semantic component at all as part of linguistic description is due to the work of Jerrold J. Katz, Jerry A. Fodor, and Paul M. Postal.[40] They worked on a semantic theory within the framework of transformational-generative linguistics. Since they also assumed the independence of meaning and syntax, they could say, at least as a first approximation, "Linguistic description minus grammar equals semantics."[41] "Grammar" here means syntax, phonology, phonemics, and morphology.

The problem that these authors are dealing with is the native speaker's ability to understand totally new sentences (out of the infinitely many possible ones) on the basis of those sentences that the speaker has happened to encounter; this is named the "projection problem." The native speaker somehow understands not only the meanings of the lexical items in the sentence but also their relationships. These authors give a few examples of the projection problem that a semantic theory should explain: structurally identical sentences may have different meanings ("the dog bit the man"; "the cat bit the woman"), or structurally different sentences may have identical meanings ("two chairs are in the room"; "there are at least two things in the room and each is a chair").[42] Also, morphologically different sentences may differ in meaning ("the tiger bit me"; "the dog bit me"), or they may have identical meanings ("the oculist examined me"; "the eyedoctor examined me"). Other aspects of the problem are the ambiguity of such sentences as "the bill is large" and the anomaly of such sentences as "he painted the walls with silent paint" as

distinguished from the structurally identical "... with red
paint" or "... with silent rollers." A semantic theory should
cope with the speaker's ability to interpret sentences in at
least these ways. On the other hand, a semantic theory does
not have to deal with how the context or the setting of the
sentence affects how it is understood; that cannot be done
without representing all the knowledge speakers have of the
world, an impossible task.[43]

The authors suggest that a semantic theory

> must contain two components: a dictionary of the
> lexical items of the language and a system of rules
> (which we shall call projection rules) which oper-
> ates on full grammatical descriptions of sentences
> and on dictionary entries to produce semantic in-
> terpretations for every sentence of the language.[44]

The "full grammatical descriptions" that are part of the input
for the projection rules are provided by the syntactic component of T-G grammar, which claims to be a model of the
speaker's internal processes and thus solves part of the projection problem. Its descriptions specify

> the elements out of which a sentence is constructed,
> the grammatical relations between those elements
> and between the higher constituents of the sentence,
> the relation between the sentence and other sentences
> of the language, and the ways the sentence is am-
> biguous together with an explanation of why it is
> ambiguous in these ways.[45]

This means, in the language of Aspects, that the deep structure of a sentence determines the relational aspects of meaning. This move to deep structure provides an explanation
for some sentences with different surface structures that
nevertheless seem to have the same meaning.

Thus, since "full grammatical descriptions" are provided by the syntactic component, the semantic component's
dictionary and projection rules need to be investigated. Katz,
Fodor, and Postal propose that each lexical entry has a normal form, which can be represented by a tree diagram, of
which this is an example for the English word "bachelor":[46]

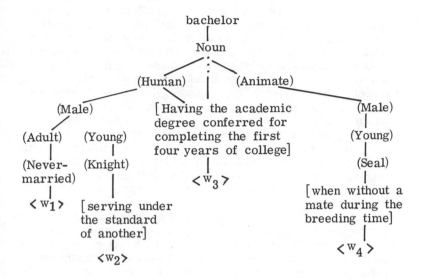

In this diagram "Noun" is a "grammatical" (or "syntactic")
marker, and the dots below it in the diagram indicate possible other syntactic markers--for example, "animate noun."
The next level, shown in parentheses--"(Male)," "(Young),"
etc.--is that of "semantic markers," which express an entry's systematic or general semantic features. Next, in
square brackets, are "distinguishers"--e.g., "[serving under
the standard of another]"--which express an entry's idiosyn-
crasies. Finally, enclosed within angles (and not spelled out
here) are the "selection restrictions," which express the conditions under which a sense may combine with others when
projection rules are applied. Each complete sequence of the
symbols represents a different sense of the entry, and is
called a "reading."

    A simplification of the dictionary can be made because
of the "category inclusion relation," when one semantic-marker
category includes another. Since, for example, "human" is
a subcategory of "animate," but not the reverse, the relation
need be stated only once at the beginning of the dictionary,
not repeated in each entry. These rules will minimize the
symbols in the dictionary, but, more importantly, they express
generalizations about the semantic properties of languages.

The second component of semantic theory is the set of projection rules. The syntactic structure of a sentence restricts how the readings may be combined, but the projection rules produce the derived meanings. The most deeply embedded constituents of the phrase structure are combined first by the projection rules; then these derived meanings are combined at the next constituent level, and so on, until the whole sentence is completed. This process is called "amalgamation," and accounts for how the meaning of the sentence is built up from the meaning of its parts. At each stage the selectional restrictions determine how many readings are possible. If all readings are eliminated at a particular constituent level, that constituent is anomalous; if only one reading remains, it is unambiguous; and if two or more readings remain, it is ambiguous in two or more ways.

This kind of projection rule was originally meant to work on the structure underlying a kernel sentence in the Structures sense, that is, a sentence that has undergone only obligatory transformations. The question of "transforms"--sentences that have undergone optional transformations--depends on whether or not such transformations are meaning-preserving. For transformations that do not change meaning, the authors suggest the convention that the transforms they produce be considered members of an "equivalence class." Every member of such an equivalence class would be interpreted in the same way as the kernel sentence underlying it. If transformations existed that changed meaning--and in 1963-64 with the "Standard Theory" imminent it looked unlikely-- a second type of projection rule would have to be devised, which would relate the interpreted phrase markers of the kernel sentences underlying such a transform. With the advent of the Standard Theory the second type of projection rule was not pursued.

The thrust of this Katz-Fodor-Postal semantic theory fit in beautifully with Chomsky's syntactic theory in Aspects, and it is a combination of the two that is called the Standard Theory. It is not the case that the two meshed exactly. For example, Chomsky's account of the lexicon differs in some details from the Katz-Fodor-Postal account: Chomsky argues that a lexical entry consists of a set of features, some phonological and some syntactic, and of a definition, and

> it can be plausibly argued [here Chomsky refers the reader to "The Structure of a Semantic Theory"] that this too consists simply of a set of features.

(Actually, the Katz-Fodor definitions are not simply sets, but it does not seem that the further structure they impose plays any role in their theory.)[47]

Chomsky also proposes to classify as "syntactic" some of what they call semantic. But he can say flatly, "Aside from terminology, I follow here the exposition in Katz and Postal (1964). In particular, I shall assume throughout that the semantic component is essentially as they describe it."[48] He accepts their basic contention that the "meaning of a sentence is based on the meaning of its elementary parts and the manner of their combination" and that

> the manner of combination provided by the surface structure is in general almost totally irrelevant to semantic interpretation, whereas the grammatical relations expressed in the abstract deep structure are, in many cases, just those that determine the meaning of the sentence.[49]

This makes an extremely elegant theory. The concept of deep structure seemed to be supported independently by both syntactic and semantic considerations; it seemed to be the input for both the transformational system (leading to the phonological component) and for the semantic component. Both the phonological component (which was fairly well worked out)[50] and the semantic component (which now seemed promisingly begun) were purely interpretive; the syntactic component provided all necessary information for both the others. It is not surprising that such symmetry carried all before it--or at any rate, enough to be called the Standard Theory.

Generative Semantics

The Standard Theory, elegant though it was, did not last very long. One of its foundations was that transformations are meaning-preserving and that therefore deep structure completely determines meaning. Soon many counter-examples were produced, among the most obvious and convincing of which were those involving logical predicates (particularly quantifiers and negatives). It was noticed, for example, that active-passive pairs of sentences with quantifiers are often not semantically equivalent--for example, "Everyone loves someone" and "Someone is loved by everyone." Even Katz and Fodor mention this particular problem, but suggest that the passive transformation might still preserve meaning "if it is true that both active and passive have the same meaning because both are ambiguous."[51] This suggestion did not find much favor, and the Standard Theory weakened under the weight of this and other objections.

Chomsky's own version of the Standard Theory never quite said that deep structure completely determined semantic interpretation; in the remark quoted on page 75 above, for example, he qualifies his statement with "in general" and "in many cases." In the same year that Aspects was published (1965) he wrote that "surface structure also contributes in a restricted but important way to semantic interpretation."[52] In any case the two functions of deep structure in the Standard Theory--as input for the transformations leading to surface structure and as input for the projection rules of the semantic component--were independent. The Extended Standard Theory (EST) as Chomsky develops it abandons the assumption that deep structure alone determines semantic interpretation; all transformations need not preserve meaning. That is, the structures that determine meaning may not be exactly the same as those from which surface structure derives. This approach to remedying the inadequacies of the Standard Theory is called the Extended Standard Theory.[53]

However, there is another approach to answering the objections to the Standard Theory, and it is called "Generative Semantics" (GS). It maintains that transformations do preserve meaning; what it changes is the character of deep structure. While of course there are differences among the linguists who represent this approach, the common factor seems to be the denial of the autonomy of syntax. George Lakoff says there is

> a general consensus in this group that semantics
> plays a central role in syntax. The generative
> semantics position is, in essence, that syntax and
> semantics cannot be separated and that the role of
> transformations, and of derivational constraints
> in general, is to relate semantic representations
> and surface structures.[54]

In particular, semantic representations and phrase markers have the same form (namely, labeled trees), and, similarly, there is no formal distinction between projection rules and grammatical transformations. Since syntax is no longer considered independent of semantics, there is no place for any distinct syntactic deep structure, especially one defined (as in the ST) as the structure after all lexical insertions have taken place but before the cyclic transformations. There may very well be intermediate levels between semantic representations and surface structure--Lakoff hypothesizes a "shallow structure" after all cyclic rules.[55] The hoped-for result is a great simplification of the model. Howard Mc-Clay's representation of the GS position looks like this:[56]

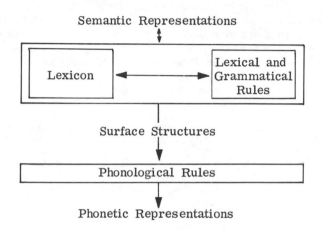

Semantic Representations

Lexicon ⟷ Lexical and Grammatical Rules

Surface Structures

Phonological Rules

Phonetic Representations

Another characteristic of generative semanticists is their relationship to symbolic logic; they tend to feel that they and logicians can help each other. Both George Lakoff and James D. McCawley, for example, want to use symbolic logic to describe semantic representations, though perhaps in an improved form. As G. Lakoff says,

> From the generative semantic point of view, the semantic representation of a sentence is a representation of its inherent logical form, as determined not only by the requirements of logic, but also by purely linguistic considerations.... Thus, it seems to me that generative semantics provides an empirical check on various proposals concerning logical form, and can be said in this sense to define a branch of logic which might appropriately be called "natural logic."[57]

McCawley argues that "symbolic logic, subject to certain modifications, provides an appropriate system for semantic representation within the framework of transformational grammar. " He adds, "I thus hold that the much-criticized title, The Laws of Thought, which George Boole gave to the first work on symbolic logic, is actually much more appropriate than has generally been thought the case. [58]   As an example McCawley takes the ambiguous sentence "Willy said that he has seen the woman who lives at 219 Main Street. "[59] The first meaning is made clear if the sentence is followed with "but the woman he has in mind really lives in Pine St. " The second interpretation emerges if the sentence is followed by "but he doesn't know that she lives there. " McCawley concludes that clauses must be separated into propositions with indices and noun phrases that identify the indices of the propositions.   Thus the first meaning of the sentence would be represented semantically as follows (where the representation is simplified to make this point):

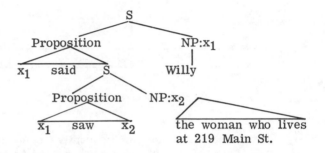

The second semantic representation would look like this:

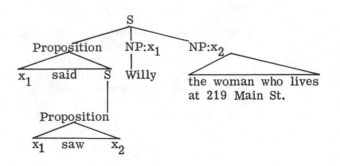

Another example of McCawley's semantic approach is his analysis of the sentence "Sam killed Pete":[60]

CAUSE BECOME NOT ALIVE where x_1 = Sam and x_2 = Pete.

Successive applications of the transformation McCawley proposes be called "Predicate raising" lead to this series of lexicalizations:

> Sam caused Pete to become not alive.
> Sam caused Pete to become dead.
> Sam caused Pete to die.
> Sam killed Pete.

Because they want to work towards systems of this sort many generative semanticists would call linguistics a branch of logic.

Among generative semanticists there is a tendency, perhaps understandable in a "second-generation" group of scholars, to emphasize their differences from Chomsky. Sometimes they talk as if their position were significantly, even radically, distinct from Chomsky's version of the EST in particular. They usually acknowledge Chomsky as the originator, in general, of the school of linguistics within which they work, or at least as the one who made it possible to formulate the questions to which they are addressing themselves with some success. McCawley, for example, describes his work as "transformational grammar" because it includes something that "has roughly the form of the 'transformational component' of a grammar as discussed in Chomsky (1965)."[61] But there is some tendency to downgrade Chomsky's contribution, particularly by G. Lakoff, who downplays Chomsky's originality and independence from Structuralism, or at least from Zellig Harris. He says, "Generative semantics is an outgrowth of transformational grammar as developed by Harris, Chomsky, Lees, Klima, Postal, and others." Later in the same article he adds,

> Early transformational grammar, as initiated by
> Harris, and developed by Chomsky, made the as-
> sumption [that syntax and semantics are independ-
> ent].... Thus, early transformational grammar
> was a natural outgrowth of American structural
> linguistics, since it was concerned with discovering
> the regularities governing the distribution of surface
> forms. [62]

This seems like calling Einstein "a natural outgrowth" of
Newtonianism, because Einstein did not reject all further
measurement of matter.   There is a sense, of course, in
which both Einstein and Chomsky are natural outgrowths of
their predecessors; few scientific theories spring full grown
from their creators' minds, without parent or genealogy.   It
is true that Chomsky has insisted on the autonomy of syntax
in relation to semantics, like structural linguistics.   But it
seems ungracious of Lakoff to ignore the really revolutionary
aspect that was present even in Chomsky's earliest work: his
insistence that the goal of linguistics is not the classification
of primary linguistic data but the development of a theory
that will provide a systematic characterization of all grammatical sentences of a language.   Whether some version of
GS or the EST--or something entirely different--proves most
useful in the long run, Lakoff himself is working on Chomsky's ground, not Harris's.   John Searle, whose sympathies
lay with the generative semanticists in 1972, who describes
them as radicals in relation to Chomsky, and who criticizes
some aspects of Chomsky's work with great vigor, insists
that the generative semanticists are building on Chomsky's
work and that the battle is being fought entirely within the
"revolutionary" conceptual system invented by Chomsky. [63]
Maclay sums up his view of the relationship:

> If this [GS] is the beginning of some sort of lin-
> guistic revolution, its magnitude should not be over-
> estimated.   The battle between Chomsky and his
> critics is being fought according to rules which
> Chomsky himself developed and is essentially a
> sectarian war among scholars who share a common
> understanding as to the general goals of linguistic
> analysis.   All agree that the aim of a linguistic
> description is to explain the relationships between
> two independently specifiable entities: sound and
> meaning.   Further, it is held that descriptions
> must contain a lexicon and that transformational
> rules which map phrase-markers onto other phrase-

markers are fundamental mechanisms of linguistic theory. Although the existence of a distinct syntactic level of deep structure may be in dispute, no one denies that a distinction has to be made between surface structures and underlying structures. This shared system of values permits confrontations of a very direct and intense sort among linguists who hold different views. [64]

Chomsky himself takes all this calmly. He seems a little surprised by the vehement expressions of independence of some of the generative semanticists, since their position seems to him largely a notational variant of the EST. To him GS seems to use different terminology but to have the same empirical outcome as the EST, and that is the crucial question. In his article "Deep Structure, Surface Structure, and Semantic Interpretation" Chomsky discusses some of the GS proposals: the proposal that at least some transformations must take place before some lexical insertions, thus eliminating traditional "deep structure" (Lakoff); the proposal that a phrase-marker might be a representation of a lexical item and could thus be replaced by that item (such as McCawley's cause-to-die = kill); and the proposal that some semantically significant relations among phrases, such as agent-action, are represented by another set of structures called "case systems" (Fillmore). [65] For each proposal Chomsky explains why he thinks that these apparent alternatives to his position are merely questions of terminology: again and again he concludes that, at least at the current level of discussion, these apparent differences do not have any empirical results. The need for empirical results, incidentally, is not in dispute; in "On GS" G. Lakoff eliminates the ST partly because its deep structure produces empirical results no different from the theory he defines and names the "Basic Theory," which does not have that deep structure.

McCawley's proposals do have empirical results that actually differ from Chomsky's. But Chomsky questions whether, first, the systems themselves are actually different, or only the realizations, which could, in that case, be translated into other systems. Second, he questions whether the realizations are better or worse, on empirical grounds, than those of the ST. He does not think the first question has yet been answered; as to the second, after examining a typical example of the alternative realizations he concludes that they are not an improvement.

All in all Chomsky does not think that GS positions
are very different from EST positions.   He says,

> Proponents of GS generally take the major bifur-
> cation to be between ST-EST and GS, and argue
> that a great deal is at stake. But many proponents
> of ST and EST, myself included, have argued that
> the central substantive issue of theory is the one
> that divides ST from EST-GS (namely, the role of
> surface structures in semantic interpretation), and
> that GS differs from EST primarily in that it re-
> laxes some of the conditions on grammars imposed
> by EST. Part of the confusion of recent debate
> perhaps results from quite different perceptions as
> to what the issues are.[66]

As to the division between semantics and syntax--if any--he
refers the reader to his discussion of the problem in Aspects.
In addition, he remarks that he himself has no particular intuition to help him decide whether a particular distinction in
grammaticalness should be classified as semantic or syntactic
and is therefore somewhat dubious about others' claims to
such intuitions.

> I suspect that they are adhering to certain tradi-
> tional explanations, which may or may not be cor-
> rect. . . . It remains, I think, an open and perhaps
> interesting question to establish sharper criteria
> that will help to make the question "syntactic or
> semantic?" more precise.[67]

In the meantime the evidence is not in, and linguists are far
from reaching a consensus comparable to the ST. Even the
extremes, EST and GS--whether they are different in fact or
merely in terminology--are far from being monolithic or even
stable. The constantly changing situation causes problems for
those who want a firm and fixed discipline, but it represents
a common stage in the development of scientific theories, and
the hope is that an even more elegant explanatory theory--
whether in GS terms, EST terms, or, perhaps more likely,
in some other terms--will replace the inadequate Standard
Theory.

Philosophy: John R. Searle

One of the most important twentieth-century movements
in philosophy is what is usually called "ordinary language

philosophy," after Ludwig Wittgenstein's remark, "Ordinary language is all right."[68] This was a change from earlier forms of linguistic philosophy, which tended to dismiss natural language as imprecise, ambiguous, and, in the extreme case of logical positivism, largely meaningless. Thus the thrust of these early philosophies was usually directed toward the construction of "improved" languages without the flaws of natural languages.

Ordinary language philosophy, on the other hand, tries to study carefully the details of a natural language. One of the leading contemporary ordinary-language philosophers is John R. Searle, whose most influential book is Speech Acts.[69] In it he defines the fundamental unit of language as a particular type of intentional act, the "speech act"--for example, promising, stating, or commanding. Speech acts are analyzed in terms of, among other things, the constitutive rules that apply between speaker and hearer (who may be the same person) in some particular context. In Searle's understanding, language is essentially communication.

In the preface to Speech Acts Searle lists those to whom he is indebted for "helpful advice and criticism"; he mentions being "especially grateful" to, among others, Noam Chomsky.[70] However, in the text itself, Chomsky's work is referred to only twice, and then merely in passing.[71] Thus the real dialog in print between Searle and Chomsky begins with Searle's 1972 article, "Chomsky's Revolution in Linguistics."[72] On the whole the article is fair and appreciative in its description of Chomsky's position, although the description of the lexicon remains, oddly, on the Structures level, with lexical items being inserted by P-S rules. But Searle emphasizes the magnitude of the changes brought about by Chomsky in philosophy and psychology, as well as in linguistics, and points out that all criticisms of Chomsky are now being carried out in terms of the framework established by Chomsky himself. "Whoever wins, the old structuralism will be the loser."[73]

Searle himself has several criticisms of Chomsky. One cluster, involving Chomsky's "Cartesianism," has been mentioned earlier.[74] But Searle's most basic objection is to Chomsky's adamant separation of semantics from syntax. In Searle's opinion this is "peculiar and eccentric." The function of language is intrinsically communication, just as the function of the heart is to pump blood, and it is "pointless and perverse" to study structure without studying

function. [75]   The GS position has as its identifying characteristic the abandonment of Chomsky's separation of syntax and
semantics, and thus Searle finds himself in sympathy with
the generative semanticists over against Chomsky. [76]

Thus Searle objects to Chomsky's work partly because
it is counterintuitive; it goes against common sense to study
language apart from its essential function, communication.
However, Searle also raises the question of the adequacy of
the semantic component in principle, as it was worked out
in the Standard Theory.   Searle points out that the details of
the semantic component were worked out not by Chomsky but
by his "colleagues at MIT, " Katz, Fodor, and Postal. [77]   But
since Chomsky has accepted this work as part of the description of language, it is legitimate to criticize it as part of
Chomsky's grammar, although he is not responsible for all
its details.   Searle claims that this theory of meaning has
the same problem that almost all theories of meaning have
had up until recently: their analyses of meaning are either
circular or inadequate.   In Chomsky's case the semantic
component takes the deep structures and assigns them a set
of readings, in terms of a semantic alphabet that is still to
be developed; each reading is a semantic representation--a
description of the meaning of the sentence.   The problem,
Searle says, is with the nature of the readings.   If they are
merely paraphrases of the sentence, the analysis is circular.
(Searle calls most examples of readings in the literature
"usually rather bad paraphrases.... We are assured that
the paraphrases are only for illustrative purposes, that they
are not the real readings.")[78]   On the other hand, if the
readings are only lists of elements, then the analysis is
inadequate; the fact that a sentence represents, for example,
a statement will not be indicated.   Semantic competence must
be more than a speaker's ability to produce and understand
new sentences; it must involve the speaker's ability to perform and understand speech acts.

> Saying something and meaning it is essentially a
> matter of saying it with the intention to produce
> certain effects on the hearer.   And these effects
> are determined by the [semantic] rules that attach
> to the sentence that is uttered. [79]

An analysis along these lines does not suffer, Searle claims,
from either circularity or inadequacy, since it does not result in either paraphrases or uninterpreted elements; the
speaker's intention holds it together.   The fact that a semantic

theory based on speech acts works, while Chomsky's semantic theory does not, is another result of the fact that a speech
acts theory recognizes the unbreakable connection between
language and communication, while Chomsky "sometimes
writes as if sentences were only incidentally used to talk
with."[80]

Searle suggests that Chomsky's preoccupation with
syntax independent of semantics is partly a holdover from
his structuralist training and partly a fear that admitting
speech acts into a theory of meaning would lead to a new
sort of behaviorism, unless, of course, speech acts are relegated to the sphere of performance rather than of competence.   But the most important reason is that Chomsky thinks
that syntax, not semantics, is determined by the biological
structure of the human brain, and therefore that the study
of syntax, not semantics, will uncover many of the innate
qualities of the human mind.   In any case, as Searle points
out, Chomsky has provided a powerful new method that has
already had a revolutionary influence on several intellectual
disciplines, even among those scholars who strongly disagree
with him.

Chomsky's side of this discussion appeared in Reflections on Language, in which he deals with Searle (and this
article) in particular and with "communication theorists" in
general.[81]   He clears up a couple of misunderstandings--he
has never suggested that there is no connection between the
structure of language and its function (including communication), or that use and structure do not influence each other[82]
--but he calls Searle's account on the whole "accurate and
compelling, including many of the critical comments."[83]
Nevertheless, he disagrees with some of Searle's conclusions.

Chomsky does not himself take up the defense of the
semantic component against Searle's charge of circularity or
inadequacy; he refers the reader to works by Katz.[84]   But
he does take up Searle's issue of communication as the essential purpose of language, and deals with an account of
meaning similar to Searle's.   Chomsky remarks that he himself considers the essential feature of language to be its creative nature, not its structure.   In this he is following a
tradition as respectable as that of the communication theorists, the tradition in which language is a system for expressing thoughts.   However, Chomsky is not sure that he
and Searle are as far apart here as Searle thinks they are.
Searle's "communication" has been enlarged to include self-

communication, which may be very much like expressing one's thoughts.   In this sense of communication it is at least partly true that the function of language is communication (although in this use the notion "communication" has lost its precision). But even if this is true, we still know nothing about the structure of language.   To take Searle's analogy of the heart, to decide that the heart's function is pumping blood tells us nothing about the structure of the heart; that remains to be investigated on its own terms.   Similarly, even if the function of language is communication, in the extended sense, we know nothing from that fact about the structure of language. In particular, we cannot leap to the conclusion that syntax is (or is not) autonomous.   Just as we can have no a priori intuition about the structure of the heart from knowing its function, neither can we have any intuition about the structure of language, one way or the other.   For example, the transformations in natural languages seem to be structure-dependent. It does not seem to be the case that this has anything to do with communication, which could occur just as well with a structure-independent language.

Thus Searle's claim about the essential connection between language and communication is true but not particularly helpful under the broad definition of communication.   However, if communication is taken in the more usual meaning, in its narrower sense, Searle's claim is simply false.   There are many ordinary instances of language uttered with no intent to communicate--perhaps because no hearer is assumed to exist.   Or in some cases it may be even stronger--a hearer is assumed not to exist.   In these cases a speaker may utter sentences that have their normal meaning, and mean what they say, but the speaker's intentions have nothing to do with their meaning.   One of Chomsky's concrete examples is his writing of what became LSLT.   "As a graduate student, " he writes,

> I spent two years writing a lengthy manuscript, assuming throughout that it would never be published or read by anyone.   I meant everything I wrote, intending nothing as to what anyone would believe about my beliefs, in fact, taking it for granted that there would be no audience.[85]

He believes that this sort of incident is commonplace in ordinary language use.   Since the supposed connection between meaning and speech acts breaks down in all these cases, it is not sufficient to support a theory of meaning.   Even when we restrict ourselves to cases in which the speaker does intend to produce some effect on the hearer, at best this approach will help with the analysis of successful communication, not with an analysis of meaning.

However, there is another weakness, according to Chomsky. All theories (including Searle's) that claim to explain meaning in terms of the speaker's intentions have always had to reintroduce "literal meaning" or "linguistic meaning" or some equivalent as unexplained notions, thus falling into circularity. Chomsky spells out the details with regard to H. P. Grice's version of a theory of meaning, not Searle's, since he considers Grice's account to be "the most careful and comprehensive effort to explain the meaning of linguistic expressions within [a speech-acts type] framework."[86] However, he thinks the same type of circularity applies to all forms of the theory of "communication-intention."[87]

The difference between Chomsky and Searle can be described (and perhaps oversimplified) by noting what each expects from the study of language. Searle expects that language study will provide some answers to important and interesting philosophical problems involving intention and communication. Chomsky insists that language did not evolve for the convenience of philosophers, and there is no guarantee that it will conform to whatever role a particular philosopher may assign to it. Its study will, however, illuminate human nature, though only on its own terms, since it is a product of the structure of the human mind (and, probably, brain), and there is no doubt that Chomsky expects this to be philosophically interesting and enlightening. But it may not answer Searle's particular questions.

Searle reviewed Reflections on Language in the article "The Rules of the Language Game,"[88] which, as far as I know, is the latest publication in the Searle-Chomsky exchange. Since it is a review, he naturally spends most of his effort on the areas of disagreement, but ends with a word or two of appreciation for the power and comprehensiveness of Chomsky's theories. He claims that Chomsky's return charge of circularity does not hold, because Chomsky dealt with Grice, not with Searle, and says that Chomsky has not shown that Searle's notion of "rules, intentions, or conditions surreptitiously contains the notion of linguistic meaning."[89] It is not clear whether he thinks that Chomsky's criticisms of Grice hold; in any case he does not explain why, if Chomsky is right about "literal meaning" being hidden in Grice's account, it is not also in Searle's own.

Searle again spends some time criticizing Chomsky's label "Cartesian" and some of the conclusions he thinks Chomsky has drawn about human freedom from it. That has been discussed above.[90] But his first major objection is to Chomsky's "rhetorical device" of a neutral scientist who, upon examining human language, comes up with such things as the structural-dependency hypothesis. Searle counters with "neutral scientist number two," who, upon examining human language, finds it necessary to deal with it as a rule-governed form of human behavior. Chomsky's neutral scientist is, Searle says, "Noam Chomsky thinly disguised and number two is the present reviewer totally undisguised."[91]

This is really only partly true. Chomsky's neutral scientist does, as Searle implies, start with certain presuppositions and questions, but they are not intended to be Chomsky's personal idiosyncratic presuppositions but those of a natural scientist, not, for example, a social scientist or a philosopher. Chomsky has tried to be consistent about this from his earliest work, and he makes it clear again when he introduces his neutral scientist: "Imagine a scientist ... who is unencumbered by the ideological baggage that forms part of our intellectual tradition and is thus prepared to study humans as organisms in the natural world."[92] The issue between Searle and Chomsky is whether this is an adequate model for studying human language. Searle thinks it is inadequate from the very beginning, that nothing of great depth can be said about language without bringing in "intention" and "rule-governed behavior" from the start. Chomsky believes that this method can lead to interesting results even though it is possible that the results may be limited. He has, personally, rather large hopes for the whole project, but is careful to add,

> It is a coherent and perhaps correct proposal that the language faculty constructs a grammar only in conjunction with other faculties of mind. If so, the language faculty itself provides only an abstract framework, an idealization that does not suffice to determine a grammar.[93]

Even if this should turn out to be the case it would still be of use to study this very abstract language faculty, as well as how it interacted with other human mental faculties.

Searle objects also to the complexity of the EST--he refers to the "large number of epicycles" now necessary[94]-- and especially to Chomsky's taking the complexity as support for his innateness theory. The rules are so complex that very small children cannot possibly "learn" them; therefore, according to Chomsky, the "rules" must be innate. Rather, Searle claims it is more plausible that the rules, as formulated by Chomsky, are wrong. Searle charges that it has never been explained how such rules guide--"as opposed to merely describe"[95]--speech. If they really did guide speech, then a speaker should recognize that they are indeed the rules that he has unconsciously been following, once they have been explained.

Here Searle misunderstands the function of a scientific model. A scientific model is an intellectual construct that intends (ideally) to be in some sort of one-to-one correspondence with whatever it is a model of; the structures that the model generates map exactly onto the system the model is describing. The model is not the system itself, but a conceptualization. It does not guide anything; it "merely describes"--as exactly as possible, with as much elegance as possible.

As an example, since 1963 the attempt has been made in physics to build up a theory of elementary particles in terms of hypothetical entities called "quarks." The observed so-called "elementary" particles were discovered to be extremely numerous and clearly complex; they are now thought to be made up of the really (perhaps) elementary quarks; there are currently supposed to be (in one version of the theory) twelve kinds of quarks, which are combinations of the three "colors" and four "flavors" (one of which has the property "charm") that quarks come in. Despite many attempts, no one has yet, as far as I know, succeeded in observing a quark experimentally. Yet the explanatory power of the model is so great that scientists are reluctant to abandon it, even though the existence of quarks is so problematic. Instead they are trying to build into the theory an explanation of why the quark should be so hard to find.[96] Of course, physicists expect that something corresponds to this hypothetical entity, the quark, however inaccessible, or the model would not be so successful. Similarly, Chomsky expects that something physical--probably largely located in the brain-- corresponds to the model of language, whether or not that "something" can ever be precisely demonstrated. Whether the rules of the theory correspond to what a speaker's introspection says is as irrelevant to this sort of theory of language as it is to the theory of quarks. The point is that the rules of Chomsky's theory of language come closer than any other theory to the ideal of generating all the grammatical sentences (and only the grammatical sentences) of language.

Of course, a scientific model is by no means sacrosanct, as the history of theories of elementary particles, for example, shows. Searle's point about epicycles is well taken. When the epicycles grow too numerous, or the elementary particles multiply beyond a reasonable point, scientists grow uncomfortable and search for a more elegant theory with equal or greater descriptive power. The one thing they do not do, of course, is move backward to a less explanatory theory.

Many people think that linguistics is in that position now, and has been moving in that direction ever since the demise of the elegant but inadequate Standard Theory. It was Chomsky's version of the EST that provoked Searle's remark about epicycles; the charge applies even more strongly to his post-1975 work, in which the transformational component has been drastically simplified at the cost of introducing enormous complexity into the PS component and thus into the system as a whole.[97] However, it is not clear that any of the competing theories (including Searle's) is, at this stage, in a stronger position. No doubt in time a new synthesis or a new theory will replace the current confusion, but it will not be a pre-Chomsky type of theory. Chomsky's revolution in linguistics cannot be undone.

Notes

[1]His theory of language appears in Verbal Behavior (New York: Appleton-Century-Crofts, 1957). Hereafter called VB.

[2]For the background to Skinner's language theory see his other works: Science and Human Behavior (New York: Macmillan, 1953; Free Press, 1965) and The Behavior of Organisms: An Experimental Analysis (New York: Appleton-Century-Crofts, 1938).

[3]VB, p. 3.

[4]Ibid. The quotation marks around "causes" (of verbal behavior) and "causal" (analysis of verbal behavior) are Skinner's own use, but he does not say what they mean. Perhaps he wants to emphasize that verbal behavior is usually the result of multiple causes, or that the effect is not exactly the occurrence of a particular instance of verbal behavior, but the probability that it will occur.

[5]Ibid., p. 6. Even a nonbehaviorist can feel some sympathy for Skinner's objections, although his solution seems to have no substance. Grammarians have "explained" oddities by naming them from early times--cf. the "hortatory subjunctive." Even structuralist linguistics merely classified; it did not explain.

[6]Ibid., p. 2.

[7]These are Skinner's examples. Ibid., p. 14.

[8]Ibid., p. 225. Skinner's italics.

[9]Ibid., p. 31.

[10]Behavior of Organisms, pp. 178-79. Quoted in Noam Chomsky, "A Review of B. F. Skinner's Verbal Behavior," Language 35 (1959): 26-58, reprinted in The Structure of Language: Readings in the Psychology of Language, J. A. Fodor and J. J. Katz, eds. (Englewood Cliffs, N.J.: Prentice-Hall, 1964), pp. 547-78. Hereafter called "Review." The Skinner quote is from p. 550, n. 2.

[11]VB, p. 41.

[12]Ibid., pp. 38-39.

[13]Ibid., p. 82.

[14]Ibid., p. 113.

[15]Ibid., p. 139.

[16]Ibid., p. 145.

[17]Ibid., pp. 434-37.

[18]Ibid., p. 227.

[19]Ibid., p. 315.

[20]Ibid., pp. 337-38, 347.

[21]Ibid., pp. 26, 352.

[22]Ibid., p. 458. It might with equal plausibility be argued that anything other than behaviorism was a more likely stimulus for "black scorpion," since Whitehead also produced the autoclitic "no" qualifying "black scorpion" in a discussion in which behaviorism was very much present.

[23]"Review." See n. 10.

[24]Ibid., p. 548, n. 1, which also includes bibliographic references.

[25]Ibid., p. 552.

[26]See above, p. 61.

[27]"Review," p. 565.

[28]Ibid., pp. 554-56; VB, p. 441.

[29]"Review," pp. 558-59; VB, pp. 224-26.

[30]"Review," p. 572.

[31]VB, p. 329.

[32]"Review," p. 574. Note 45 adds: "One might just as well argue that exactly the opposite is true," and cites some evidence.

[33]Chomsky does not deal with this, but Skinner is very old-fashioned in his view of an ideal language, also. For him an ideal language is one in which there is a one-to-one correspondence between the language and objects (stimuli). For example, "The word for two houses alike except for color would be alike except for the element referring to color." (VB, p. 123). He admits that the ideal language is impossible, but the more a language can separate and manipulate individual units of response, the closer to the ideal it is. This "picture theory" of language dominated the field from earliest times until Wittgenstein's conversion from his Tractatus period.

[34]VB, p. 11.

[35]See above, p. 67.   Probably even Skinner did not differentially reinforce his children in all the nuances of English pronunciation.

[36]"Review," p. 563; note 31 contains some bibliographic references.

[37]Ibid., p. 577.

[38]Aspects, p. 159.

[39]Ibid., p. 163.

[40]J. J. Katz and J. A. Fodor, "The Structure of a Semantic Theory," Language 39 (1963): 170-210. Reprinted in The Structure of Language, pp. 469-518. J. J. Katz and P. M. Postal, An Integrated Theory of Linguistic Descriptions (Cambridge, Mass.: MIT Press, 1964).

[41]"Structure of a Semantic Theory," p. 483.

[42]These and the following examples are from "The Structure of a Semantic Theory," pp. 483-85.

[43]Katz and Fodor add: "For practically any item of information about the world, the reader will find it a relatively easy matter to construct an ambiguous sentence whose resolution in context requires the representation of that item." The authors have made this the basis of a parlor game. "Although this game is not remarkably amusing, it is surprisingly convincing." "Structure of a Semantic Theory," p. 489, and n. 9.

[44]"Structure of a Semantic Theory," p. 493.

[45]Ibid., p. 483.

[46]An Integrated Theory of Linguistic Descriptions, p. 14.

[47]Aspects, p. 214, n. 15.   See also above, pp. 34-35.

[48]Ibid., p. 198, n. 10.

[49]Ibid., p. 162.

[50]See Ibid., p. 198, n. 10, in which Chomsky lists some works that describe the phonological component.

[51]"The Structure of a Semantic Theory," p. 515, n. 27.

[52]Language and Mind, p. 126.   He credits the work of Jackendoff with convincing him of this.

[53]For Chomsky's version of EST see above, pp. 42 ff.

[54]George Lakoff, "On Generative Semantics," in Semantics: An Interdisciplinary Reader in Philosophy, Linguistics, and Psychology, Danny D. Steinberg and Leon A. Jakobovits, eds. (Cambridge, England: Cambridge University Press, 1971), p. 232, n. a.   This article by G. Lakoff will hereafter be called "On GS," and the Steinberg and Jakobovits book will be called Semantics.   Lakoff lists himself, Postal, Fillmore, Ross, McCawley, Bach, R. Lakoff, Perlmutter, "and others" as linguists who take a GS position, although of course with differences of detail; for purposes of this discussion I am taking G. Lakoff and McCawley as typical representatives.

[55]"On GS," p. 283.

[56]Howard Maclay, "Overview," in Semantics, p. 177.

[57]"On GS," p. 277.

[58]James D. McCawley, "Where Do Noun Phrases Come From?," in Semantics, p. 219.

[59]This example and its diagrams are from "Where Do Noun Phrases Come From?," pp. 224-25.

[60]This example is a somewhat simplified version of McCawley's work in "Lexical Insertion in a Transformational Grammar," in Papers from the 4th Regional Meeting of the Chicago Linguistic Society, April 1968.   This version of it is actually taken from John T. Grinder and Suzette Haden Elgin, Guide to Transformational Grammar: History, Theory, Practice (New York: Holt, Rinehart and Winston, 1973), pp. 160-62.   I have altered it slightly in the interests of consistency.

[61]"Where Do Noun Phrases Come From?," p. 217.

[62]"On GS," p. 232, n. a; pp. 267-68.

[63]John R. Searle, "Chomsky's Revolution in Linguistics," The New York Review of Books, 1972.   Reprinted in On Noam Chomsky, p. 18.

[64]"Overview," p. 178.   A footnote (n. a, same page) points out that even the structure of the argumentation in Lakoff's "On GS" imitates Chomsky's.

[65]"Deep Structure, Surface Structure, and Semantic Interpretation," p. 157, pp. 188-89, and pp. 190-91, respectively.

[66]Reflections on Language, p. 238, n. 2.   As if to illustrate this last sentence, G. Lakoff says, "On the whole I would say that the discussion of surface and intermediate structure interpretation rules found in Chomsky, Jackendoff, and Partee do not [sic] deal with the real issues."   "On GS," p. 267.

[67]Reflections on Language, p. 95.

[68]Ludwig Wittgenstein, The Blue and Brown Books (New York: Harper & Row, 1958), p. 28.

[69]John R. Searle, Speech Acts: An Essay in the Philosophy of Language (Cambridge, England: Cambridge University Press, 1969).

[70]Also to Julian Boyd. Speech Acts, p. [vii].

[71]Speech Acts, p. 14, n. 1, and p. 64.

[72]John R. Searle, "Chomsky's Revolution in Linguistics," The New York Review of Books, 1972.   Reprinted in On Noam Chomsky, pp. 2-33.   Hereafter called "Chomsky's Revolution."

[73]Ibid., p. 18.

[74]See above, p. 40.

[75]"Chomsky's Revolution," p. 16.

[76]Apparently it is this sympathy that leads him into a curious claim.   He characterizes Chomsky's revolution as an example of the American academic "Young Turk" phenomenon, and the GS movement as a second generation "Young Turk"

movement, with Chomsky now the Old Turk. (Searle mentions, but apparently does not agree with, Chomsky's opinion that the apparent differences between GS and EST are largely terminological). Searle claims at least four times in "Chomsky's Revolution" that "many of Chomsky's best students" have become generative semanticists (pp. 8, 15, and twice on p. 17). On p. 17 Searle lists as examples of the GS position Ross, Postal, G. Lakoff, McCawley, and Fillmore ("some of these are among [Chomsky's] best students"). Of this list, as far as I can find out, only Ross did his work at MIT and thus could have been Chomsky's student. Postal was certainly an early disciple, but not a student in the strict sense. Maclay makes a similar claim, although only once, in "Overview," p. 165. However, he mentions only G. Lakoff, Fillmore, and McCawley, none of whom were Chomsky's students. Of the three other generative semanticists in G. Lakoff's list (above, p. 94, n. 54), only one, Perlmutter, studied at MIT.

77"Chomsky's Revolution," p. 23.

78Ibid., p. 27.

79Ibid., p. 29.

80Ibid., pp. 29-30.

81Reflections on Language, esp. pp. 53-77.

82Ibid., p. 56.

83Ibid., p. 235, n. 27.

84Katz has argued against circularity in Semantic Theory (New York: Harper & Row, 1972) and in "Logic and Language: An Examination of Recent Criticism of Intentionalism," in Minnesota Studies in Philosophy of Science, vol. 6, Gunderson, Keith, and Grover, eds. (Minneapolis: University of Minnesota Press, 1975). His critique of Searle appears in Propositional Structure and Illocutionary Force: A Study of the Contribution of Sentence Meaning to Speech Acts (Hassocks, England: Harvester, 1977).

85Reflections on Language, p. 61.

86Ibid., p. 73. Chomsky is referring particularly to H. P. Grice, "Utterer's Meaning and Intentions," Philosophical Review 78 (1969): 147-77, and to Grice, "Utterer's Meaning, Sentence-Meaning, and Word-Meaning," Foundations of Language 4 (1968): 225-42.

[87]Reflections on Language, pp. 64, 68.

[88]Times Literary Supplement, London, 10 September 1976. Hereafter called "Rules."

[89]"Rules," Section III.

[90]See above, p. 40.

[91]"Rules," Section I.

[92]Reflections on Language, p. 139. Emphasis mine.

[93]Ibid., p. 41.

[94]"Rules," Section I.

[95]Ibid., Section II.

[96]For popular discussions of quark theory see Sheldon Lee Glachow, "Quarks with Color and Flavor," Scientific American 223 (October 1975): 38-50, and Yoichiro Nambu, "The Confinement of Quarks," Scientific American 225 (November 1976): 48-60. The Nambu article deals with some proposals to cope with the unexpected difficulty in observing quarks, and ends (p. 60) rather plaintively:

> Quarks are a product of theoretical reasoning. They were invented at a time when there was no direct evidence of their existence.... Now theories of quark confinement suggest that all quarks may be permanently inaccessible and invisible. The very successes of the quark model lead us back to the question of the reality of quarks. If a particle cannot be isolated or observed, even in theory, how will we ever be able to know that it exists?

[97]Of course, this change is not capricious or unmotivated, but it seems unfortunate, especially in the light of Chomsky's early remarks about an evaluation criterion of linguistic theory being the simplicity of the system as a whole, not just a part of it.

Chapter IV

LANGUAGE AND THEOLOGY

Applying the above discussion of transformational-generative
linguistics to the theological enterprise, past and present,
might seem somewhat farfetched. However, even before
linguistics became a separate discipline theologians have been
concerned with their use of language. Some, like Augustine
and Donald Evans, have explicitly discussed the nature of
language independently of their theological application of it.
Others, like Thomas Aquinas and Paul Tillich, have shown
their understanding of language as it has come up almost
incidentally in their theological work. It is certainly true
that Christian theologians have worked, over the centuries,
in an amazing number of different ways, with a bewildering
diversity. Yet despite the genuine differences, all the ways
have at least one thing in common: they are all struggling
(explicitly or implicitly) with the problem of what language
is appropriate to describe Christian faith. Not all theologians
are explicit about this aspect of their work, and probably
most of those who are would say that appropriate language
is only a part of their concern. Nevertheless, whatever else
individual theologians do, they work with language. In modern terms theology is--at least--a linguistic discipline. If
this is the case, it is plausible that a new understanding of
language, as provided by transformational-generative linguistics, will illuminate past and contemporary theologies.

To support the claim that theology has always been at least implicitly a linguistic discipline, the following examples will illustrate the importance of language for a sampling of Christian theologians. The first is Augustine. He was a theologian for whom language was very important--perhaps not surprisingly, since he taught rhetoric as his profession before his conversion. Remarks about language occur with some frequency in his Confessions. [1] Although his description of language is not systematic, it is clear that his picture of language is centered on words. He describes how he learned language as a child, not by "some set method of teaching" (Augustine is much more sophisticated than B. F. Skinner), but by "using my mind":

> [I observed that] my elders would make some particular sound, and as they made it would point at or move towards some particular thing: and from this I came to realize that the thing was called by the sound they made when they wished to draw my attention to it. That they intended this was clear from the motions of their body, by a kind of natural language common to all races which consists in facial expressions, glances of the eye, gestures, and the tones by which the voice expresses the mind's state--for example whether things are to be sought, kept, thrown away, or avoided. So, as I heard the same words again and again properly used in different phrases, I came gradually to grasp what things they signified; and forcing my mouth to the same sounds, I began to use them to express my own wishes. [2]

When Augustine compares the ease with which he learned Latin with his difficulty in learning Greek, in both cases he identifies learning the language with learning the words. The only difference is the method of teaching. He learned Latin "amidst the flatterings of nurses and the jesting and pleased laughter of elders leading me on," but Greek was taught with "the painful pressure of compulsion. "[3]

In most cases the words and their subject matter can be separated. Augustine remarks about literature (which can lead people into sin and error): "I make no accusation against the words, which in themselves are choice and precious vessels, but against the wine of error that is in them. "[4] In this respect the two bishops who most influenced Augustine make an interesting contrast. Augustine admired the style

and words of both Faustus the Manichee and Ambrose the
Catholic. He approached Faustus expecting to receive answers to his questions, and Faustus disappointed him. He
was able

> to distinguish between it [Faustus's style] and the
> truth for which I was then so hungry. I was con-
> cerned not with the dish, but with such knowledge
> as this Faustus, of whom they thought so highly,
> might set before me to feed upon, [5]

and Faustus provided no such food. On the other hand, Augustine approached Ambrose out of interest in his style only;
he "did not take great heed to learn what he was saying."
But "while I was opening my heart to learn how eloquently
he spoke, I came to feel ... how truly he spoke."[6] In this
case, form and content, though distinguishable, were not
separable.

  After his conversion Augustine gave up his first attempt at reading Isaiah, putting it aside until he should be
"more practised in the Lord's way of speech."[7] Yet there
was for Augustine more than one style of speech possible
for Christians, at least up to a point. For Augustine the
principal such style was found in "some books of the Platonists" (i.e., Neo-Platonists). He explains that in these
books he found equivalents to some Christian theological
statements--he quotes from John 1 and Philippians 2--though
"not in the very words, yet the thing itself."[8] The words
of the "Platonists" are correct, as far as they go; it is only
that they are not complete, since they omit the crucial fin-
ish, an equivalent to "The Word was made flesh and dwelt
among us." Although Augustine does not explicitly say so
in the Confessions, the remedying of that defect was the theological task he set himself: expressing the Christian faith
in neo-Platonic language.

  The second example is St. Thomas Aquinas. I do not
know whether he ever discusses language in general and its
connection with theology, but he does distinguish different
functions of language in a discussion of whether the Eucharistic formulas--"This is my body," "This is the chalice of
my blood"--are really "true."[9] Thomas has previously established that "the power of changing which is found in the formal part of these sacramental signs, depends on the sign
fully signifying, and that only happens at the utterance of the
last syllable."[10] If this is so, then it can be argued that at

the instant the word "this" is spoken, since transubstantiation
has not yet taken place, "this" must refer to the substance
of the bread, and thus the formula is false.

Thomas considers and rejects several previous attempts to deal with the difficulty of the reference of "this."
Some theologians have taken the reference to be to "something we are thinking about," but Thomas says that if there
is "no reference to any present bodily material," then there
is no sacrament, and, in any case, the difficulty of reference
would just be moved back to Christ's original utterance of
the words.[11] Other theologians consider the reference to be
to "what is descried by our intelligence," but this is heresy,
since then the body of Christ is present only in a sign, not
in truth.[12] Others say that the reference of "this" can be
postponed, so to speak, until the last syllable of the phrase
has been uttered, and then its referent will be, not the substance of the bread, but the body of Christ. But then the
formula would mean "My body is my body," which is true,
but which was true before the words were spoken. So that
cannot be the meaning of the phrase.[13]

    To solve the problem Thomas takes an analogy from
Aristotle: "the spoken words correspond to ideas."[14] But
a distinction can be made: ideas in our "practical intelligence" actually bring something into being; ideas in our
"speculative intelligence" arise from the impact of reality.
By making the analogy one sees that the words of the Eucharistic formulas do not correspond to the ideas in the speculative intelligence; they do not presuppose what they signify.
Rather they are like ideas in the practical intelligence; they
cause what they signify. In John L. Austin's much later
terminology they are "performatives."[15] The difficult "this"
still refers, and it refers successfully, but as a pronoun,
"signifying the substance in a vague way, without qualifying
it, and leaving it without any determinate form."[16] Thus the
truth of the statement depends on its success (or its "felic-
ity," in Austin's language) as a performative.

    The next example, Paul Tillich, deals with the relation
of language and theology to some extent, although his primary
concern is with the relation of philosophy and theology. He
says that he is deliberately using nontraditional language, and
using it in a nontraditional way, in order to "speak under-
standably to the large group of educated people, including
open-minded students of theology, for whom traditional language has become irrelevant." He admits the danger, which

must be risked, that "in this way the substance of the Christian message may be lost."[17] But the mere fact of language change does not in itself make a theological statement invalid.

Much irresponsible theological language, in Tillich's opinion, comes from theologians not recognizing the philosophical origins of much of their language. It is true that the use of language is one form (among many others) of "prephilosophy," out of which philosophy developed. But since the development of philosophy, there has been a circular process: "the language of nonphilosophical literature and common usage, which is a form of prephilosophy too, is determined by previous philosophical usage," as is even antiphilosophical language.[18] A theologian does not have to use traditional language, but he does have to use philosophically examined language. "No theologian should be taken seriously as a theologian ... if his work shows that he does not take philosophy seriously." If he does not, he will succumb to the "black magic" of words.[19]

It is perhaps significant that Tillich mentions language more frequently in his later work than in his earlier; for example, the index to volume I of his Systematic Theology (1951) has only two entries for "language," while the index to volume III (1963) has sixteen. In any case theologians in recent years have become more conscious--sometimes self-conscious--about the implications of their choice of language. One of the most influential theologians in this respect has been Rudolf Bultmann. Bultmann's ideas about the relation between language and theology will be dealt with more fully below;[20] for the moment it is enough to point out that for Bultmann the theological task "consists of unfolding that understanding of God, and hence of the world and man, which arises from faith." The unfolding consists of theological statements, which "can never be the object of faith; they can only be the explication of the understanding which is inherent in faith itself."[21] Every such attempt at explication, however, is limited by the theologian's situation, including his or her language and conceptual system, and thus can never be done once and for all. "Every theological exposition ... is constructed with the use of contemporary conceptions."[22] Bultmann's own work was largely concerned with two types of language, one that was contemporary with much of the New Testament and is technically termed "mythology," and one that was contemporary with Bultmann, and is technically termed "existentialism." Bultmann's theology explicitly tried to translate the one into the other.

Within the past twenty years a number of theologians
have tried to use Ordinary Language Philosophy as a means
to do theology. Ordinary Language Philosophy is the name
given to the philosophy of language that developed out of Ludwig Wittgenstein's work after his conversion from his Tractatus Logico-Philosophicus approach to language. John L.
Austin was another major shaper of Ordinary Language Philosophy. An attempt both to further Ordinary Language Philosophy and to apply it to theological discourse was made by
Donald Evans in The Logic of Self-Involvement.[23] Evans
worked with Austin at Oxford, and Part I of the book takes
Austin's performatives as a starting point for a further analysis of "self-involving" elements in ordinary language, that
is, "the various ways in which language may involve a speaker
in something more than a bare assent to facts."[24] This
analysis is an autonomous effort in Ordinary Language Philosophy; it does not deal with religious language in particular.
Part II applies Evans's analysis to one particular example
of Christian self-involving language (and all language of faith
is self-involving): to Christian language about creation. He
remarks that what he proposes to do is make a study of
meaning, not truth; the question of truth is vital, but "questions of meaning should precede questions of truth."[25] "Ordinary language," when used about Christianity, means Biblical language; therefore Evans investigates Biblical language
about creation.

Another theologian who used Ordinary Language Philosophy, and who mediated it to many other theologians, was
Ian T. Ramsey, later Bishop of Durham, whose Religious
Language appeared in 1957. One of Ramsey's leading questions is about what language is "appropriate currency" for
religious situations.[26] Religious language is one type of
"odd" language--language with odd logical behavior--which is
necessary to evoke the characteristic "discernment" and "commitment" of the religious situation--for the "penny to drop,"
as Ramsey is fond of saying.[27] Religious language should
not be measured by the standards of other types of language--
for example, by the standards of scientific language--but only
by its own odd logic.

Paul M. Van Buren is another recent theologian who
is explicitly concerned with theological language. He made
what he later considered to be a false start, in which, using
and misunderstanding Wittgenstein and Ramsey, he identified
meaning as function with a modified verification principle,
and concluded that language about God is meaningless.[28]

Later, however, he decided that his error was thinking that
language about God functioned like everyday language. He
moved to a metaphor: language is like a platform on which
we stand to speak. We are quite safe on the "great central
plains" of ordinary speech. But we may go near the edge--
possibly even add a plank or two to the platform--where language is stretched in odd and unusual ways. If we fall off
the platform, we fall into nonsense. Theological language,
taking place so near to the edge of the platform, is always
in the double danger of falling off the platform into nonsense,
or of being taken literally, as if it belonged to the center.
The word that religion uses to describe its precarious position is "God"--"the word that is religion's peculiar way of
acknowledging the final limit of its language."29

    As final examples of theologians who deal explicitly
with the relation of theology and language, there are the
Roman Catholics Leslie Dewart and his critic Bernard J. F.
Lonergan, S. J. Dewart's concern is with what he calls the
"dehellenization of dogma," particularly what might be better called the "desupernaturalization" of the Christian doctrines of the Trinity and of Christ. The problem has arisen
because "human experience in general has become aware of
its historical character."30 Therefore dogmatic statements
couched in language developed out of an earlier human experience, which was not aware of its historical character, are
likely to be understood as false or meaningless by contemporary experience. Our experience, to Dewart, is the immediate reality that we encounter--our personal consciousness--
but this is always, for human beings, "cast in the concepts
by which we represent our personal consciousness both to
ourselves and to others," and it is exactly this "conceptualization of experience which makes man conscious and human."31 No one particular conceptualization is needed for
human experience, but human experience does require some
concrete conceptual system--which is supplied, through language, to individuals by their culture. "It follows from this
that concepts and conceptual systems (languages, cultural
forms) are translatable, but not equivalent."32 He sums up:
"To master the 'language' of contemporary experience is to
think in contemporary concepts--and to think in new concepts
is to develop one's original experience."33 Thus the proper
way to language Christian belief in God and to retain the adequacy which the "hellenic" languaging had in its time is to
begin with "not the idea that although we do not experience
God he must be nonetheless Being, but the observation that
we do experience God, although evidently we do not experience him as being."34

Bernard Lonergan criticizes sharply much of Dewart's work, both his analyses of the problem and his suggestions for a solution.   But he agrees with Dewart on the necessity for examining and changing traditional dogmatic language where necessary.   One must move from "childish realism" to "critical realism."   Under present circumstances--namely, the "disorientation of contemporary experience"--theology must change, and not in only one way.

> The popular theology devised in the past for the simplices fideles has been replaced.   Nor will some single replacement do; for theology has to learn to speak in many modes and on many levels and even to minister to the needs of those afflicted with philosophical problems they are not likely to solve.[35]

A new language, or languages, may be needed.

Thus the importance of language for doing theology has emerged with great clarity in recent theological work of many different types.   It has in fact always been true and has been seen here and there in the past.   Hence a new understanding of language is a promising development for the study of theology, and the rest of this work will try to develop two aspects of that promise.

Notes

[1]Augustine, The Confessions of Saint Augustine, trans. F. J. Sheed (London and New York: Sheed & Ward, 1011).

[2]Ibid., I.8.   This passage, incidentally, is quoted by Ludwig Wittgenstein at the beginning of his Philosophical Investigations, trans.   G. E. M. Anscombe, 2d ed.   (New York: Macmillan, 1958), § 1, to contrast the word-based interpretation of language with the approach that he himself will develop (subsequently called "Ordinary Language Philosophy").

[3]Ibid., I.14.   His conclusion has a modern ring: "Free curiosity is of more value in learning than harsh discipline."

[4]Ibid., I.16.

[5]Ibid., V.3.

[6]Ibid., V.13, 14.

[7]Ibid., IX.5.

[8]Ibid., VII.9.

[9]Thomas Aquinas, Summa Theologiae, vol. 58: The Eucharistic Presence (3a. 73-78), ed. William Barden, O.P. (Blackfriars; New York: McGraw-Hill; London: Eyre & Spottiswoode, 1965), 3a. 78, 5; pp. 187-91. Hereafter called ST.

[10]Ibid., 3a. 78, 4; p. 185.

[11]Ibid., 3a. 78, 5; p. 187.

[12]Ibid., p. 189.

[13]Ibid.

[14]Aristotle, De Interpretatione I, 1.16a3; quoted by Thomas, ST 3a. 78, 5; p. 189.

[15]John L. Austin, How to Do Things with Words, 2d ed. (Cambridge, Mass.: Harvard University Press, 1975). Thomas seems to be one of those mentioned on p. 18 above, n. 3, who work out of a more-than-referential understanding of language.

[16]ST 3a. 78, 5; p. 191.

[17]Paul Tillich, Systematic Theology, 3 vols. (Chicago: University of Chicago Press, 1951-63; Phoenix Edition, 1971), 3:4.

[18]Paul Tillich, Biblical Religion and the Search for Ultimate Reality (Chicago: University of Chicago Press, 1964), p. 10.

[19]Ibid., pp. 7-8. The words "black magic" are in quotation marks in the original, although no references are given, perhaps because the book is a slightly expanded version of Tillich's 1951 James W. Richard Lectures at the University of Virginia. The words seem to be a reference to Wittgenstein's Verhexung: "Philosophy is a battle against

the bewitchment of our intelligence by means of language."
Philosophical Investigations, § 109.

[20]See below, pp. 115-16.

[21]Rudolf Bultmann, Theology of the New Testament, 2
vols., trans. Kendrick Grobel (New York: Charles Scribner's Sons, 1951 and 1955), 2: 237-38.

[22]Rudolf Bultmann, Faith and Understanding, trans.
Louise Pettibone Smith, ed. Robert W. Funk (New York and
Evanston: Harper & Row, 1966), p. 279.

[23]Donald Evans, The Logic of Self-Involvement: A
Philosophical Study of Everyday Language with Special Reference to the Christian Use of Language About God as Creator (London: SCM Press, 1963).

[24]Ibid., p. 14.

[25]Ibid., p. 24.

[26]Ian T. Ramsey, Religious Language: An Empirical
Placing of Theological Phrases (New York: Macmillan, 1957),
p. 5.

[27]Ibid., p. 20 and elsewhere.

[28]Paul M. Van Buren, The Secular Meaning of the Gospel, Based on an Analysis of Its Language (New York: Macmillan, 1963).

[29]Paul M. Van Buren, The Edges of Language: An
Essay in the Logic of a Religion (New York: Macmillan,
1972), p. 130.

[30]Leslie Dewart, The Future of Belief: Theism in a
World Come of Age (New York: Herder & Herder, 1966), p.
79.

[31]Ibid., pp. 101, 105.

[32]Ibid., p. 106.

[33]Ibid., p. 109.

[34]Leslie Dewart, "God and the Supernatural," The Commonweal 85 (Feb. 10, 1967):   523-28; reprinted in New Theology No. 5, ed. Martin E. Marty and Dean G. Peerman (New York: Macmillan, 1968), p. 155.

[35]Bernard J. F. Lonergan, S.J., "The Dehellenization of Dogma," Theological Studies 28 (June 1967):   336-51; reprinted in New Theology No. 5, p. 175.

Chapter V

THEOLOGICAL AND RELIGIOUS PLURALISM

The Primacy of Deep Structure

The theologians reviewed above--and, it can be claimed, all
other theologians--shared a common concern for the appro-
priateness of their language, but they did not work out of a
common understanding of the nature of language or of its relation to their theology. The rest of this paper will be concerned with the development and application of the transformational-generative understanding of language already described

To recapitulate, the deep structure of a language is
generated by the base (the phrase-structure rules and the
lexicon) and is then acted upon by the operations called transformations; the result is the surface structure. The same
deep structure may, and usually does, have several surface
structures that correspond to it, depending on exactly which
transformations are used. The plurality of surface structures
associated with each deep structure will show the same "thematic relations" among their elements, but may differ in
other respects, including those aspects of meaning that are
functions of the surface structure, according to the Extended
Standard Theory. Thus the diversity of surface structures
possible from one deep structure can exhibit a fuller meaning from that deep structure than only one sequence of trans-

formations (a single surface structure) can do. In this sense the deep structure is primary, but the pluralism of surface structures is beneficial. This diversity of surface structure in relation to deep structure is characteristic of all human language.

Apparently this pluralism of surface structures as compared to deep structure is true of human institutions other than language. The structures of a culture or a society, both institutional structures and belief structures, have been related to a single underlying structure in the work of Georges Dumézil and Emile Benveniste, who build on a foundation laid by Emile Durkheim. Durkheim proposed that the religious structures of a society--the beliefs, the epics and myths, the cultic structures--are a projection of the institutional structures, including the moral structures, of the society. "Religious representations are collective representations which express collective realities."[1] These collective representations impinge upon each member of the society apparently from the outside; from the individual point of view they seem to be transcendent, and are then personified, objectified, and mythologized as external powers. Sociology, in Durkheim's opinion, now has the ability to investigate what lies under the personifications and objectifications and to lay bare the communal institutional structures that underlie the religious structures.

Dumézil made a major shift in the relationship between social structures and belief structures as proposed by Durkheim. They are still related to one another, but in a much more complex way. Rather than the one deriving from the other, as Durkheim has it, Dumézil suggests that both are derived from a more abstract underlying structure, which he names "ideology." Myths, sagas, and religious beliefs in general, as well as the social organization of a society, reflect the common ideology of that society. Dumézil has worked out what he believes to be the common ideology of parent- or Proto-Indo-European society. He claims that elements of that ideology were carried by the Indo-European (I-E) migrations across what became the I-E-speaking world and were preserved in most I-E myths and social organizations, from India to Iceland, and that this particular ideology is unique to I-E cultures.[2] He began working out this tripartite ideology in a 1930 article about the prehistoric Indo-Iranian caste system;[3] here he was greatly helped by the independent conclusions of Emile Benveniste, published in 1932,[4] which confirmed the tripartite character of ancient Iranian

society. Benveniste "had a profound influence on the development of Dumézil's ideas," and he has acknowledged it frequently. [5]

The ideology that was spread by the I-E migrations
was hierarchical and tripartite, with a particular relationship
among the strata. Dumézil calls each stratum a "function,"
meaning both an ideological principle and its representation
in the social and religious systems. The lowest and least
regarded function was that of the promotion of physical well-
being, represented in society by the herders and cultivators
who provided sustenance for the higher functions. In the religious system this stratum is represented by gods who promote fertility and great harvests, usually a pair of twins or
close relatives, and often with a female figure associated
with them. The second stratum was that of the warrior and
the military, including the ruler; it represented physical force.
In mythology there was a group of warlike gods, and gods of
physical strength. Dumézil expresses it as the stratum of
"le jeu de la vigueur physique, de la force, principalment
mais non uniquement guerrière." The top of the hierarchy,
the sovereign stratum, has two separate but co-sovereign
parts: juridical or legal sovereignty (the maintenance of
proper order among human beings) and magico-religious or
cosmic sovereignty (the maintenance of proper order among
other aspects of the universe). This stratum is that of
"l'administration à la fois mystérieuse et régulière du mon-
de," [6] and was represented by the priestly class at the top
of the social system, where they served as legal arbiters
as well as religious practitioners. In the pantheon the stratum was represented by a pair of sovereign gods.

In summary, the structure of I-E ideology, in descend-
ing order, is pictured as follows:

(1). Sovereignty: Magico-religious/juridical
(2). Force
(3). Nourishment

This pattern and this hierarchy is projected, in Dumézil's
view, into both the institutional structures and the belief structures of ancient I-E societies. Some of his examples are
given here. [7] First, his analysis of the patterns of ancient
India:

Gods	Castes
(1). Varuna/Mitra	(1). Brahmans
(2). Indra	(2). Kṣatriyas
(3). the Aśvins, Sarasvatī	(3). Vaiśyas

In Rome the three functions were represented in society, but not in the class system, which to some degree cut across them. But the three functions show up again in the myths of early Rome, the kings and tribes, later historicized:

Gods	Origins	Tribes
(1). Jupiter/Dius Fidius	(1). Romulus/Numa	(1). Ramnes
(2). Mars	(2). Tullus Hostilius	(2). Luceres
(3). Quirinus, Ops	(3). Sabines	(3). Titienses

In the German pantheon the tripartite system shows up again:

(1). Othinn/Tȳr
(2). Thōrr
(3). Njorthr, Freyr

Dumézil's concentration has been on ancient societies. C. Scott Littleton comments:

> In recent years, Dumézil has insisted that the presence of the tripartite ideology does not necessarily imply the presence of a tripartite social system.... Admittedly the evidence (outside of India) for social tripartition is far less certain than that for supernatural tripartition.[8]

Littleton, an anthropologist, goes further than Dumézil apparently would; he suggests that the I-E ideology is still active, at least in some respects, for example, the "tendency to divide phenomena into three segments, stages, or levels, which has been fundamental to Western thought since well before Aristotle, is still very much with us."[9] In this spirit Littleton applies Dumézil's theories rather widely; his justification is that the theories "in the last analysis ... are concerned with the extent to which a common linguistic heritage is necessarily accompanied by a common social and cultural heritage."[10] That there may be a relationship between language and "ideology" (or some equivalent) was recognized before Dumézil, for example, by Edward Sapir and by Benjamin Lee Whorf. Whorf, in particular, describes the way in which the Hopi language shapes the Hopi's perceptions of reality. [11] Littleton himself, following others, suggests the presence of a quadripartite ideology among Crow speakers and the Siouan-family speakers, and possibly also among the speakers of the Uto-Aztecan family. [12] Littleton also makes several suggestions about more recent or even contemporary manifestations of the I-E tripartite system among more modern I-E speakers: corresponding to sovereignty, force, and nourishment there are the three branches of the United States government (judicial = Supreme Court, executive = President, legislative = Congress), the Christian Trinity (Father, Son, Spirit), [13] the three estates of medieval society, and various tripartite schemes of thought (Hegel's thesis, antithesis, synthesis; Comte's "law of three stages," and even the tendency of anecdotes to have three parts, the first incident, the second incident, and the punch line). Dumézil seems rather cautious about these wide-ranging applications of his theory, but he does not rule them out. [14]

Apparently Dumézil is not greatly concerned with finding a label for his method. Others, including Claude Lévi-Strauss, have labeled him a Structuralist, because of his concern with underlying patterns. [15] However, even Littleton considers Dumézil an unconventional Structuralist, and his oddness stems ultimately from his emphasis on I-E ideology, even in cases when there is no "common denominator" in the material being considered. [16] Perhaps the oddness is that Dumézil's underlying pattern is precisely not a common denominator found explicitly in the myths or social structures themselves; rather it is an abstract structure that is never found in its pure state but only in a plurality of embodiments in belief structures and institutional structures. Therefore Dumézil's theory seems to have the same sort of structure as Chomsky's theory of language, with "ideology" corresponding to "deep structure" and the myths and social structures corresponding to surface structures that have undergone different transformations.

In this terminology Dumézil is saying that cultures with a common I-E language heritage have in common a particular hierarchical tripartite ideology (as described above), which is expressed in their mythologies (and epics and sagas and other belief structures) and in their social structures and institutions. In transformational-generative terms [17] the language generates the deep structure (called "ideology" by Dumézil). Then various culture-specific transformations map the ideology into various myths and theologies on the one hand, and various other culture-specific transformations map the ideology into social structures and institutions on the other hand.

In diagram form the structure would look like this:[18]

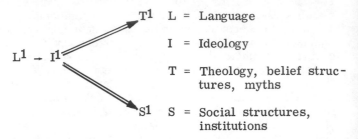

T^1 L = Language

$L^1 \rightarrow I^1$ I = Ideology

T = Theology, belief structures, myths

S^1 S = Social structures, institutions

Both myths and social institutions are surface structures, in this model, and exhibit all the richness and variety of surface structures. While the language or language family (say, I-E) may generate the same ideology, the transformations will vary from culture to culture, producing different surface structures. It may also be the case that a choice of transformations might be available within some one culture, allowing a variety of surface structures to exist within that one culture, but all deriving from the same deep structure. If this is so, the multiplicity of surface structures would together show richer interpretations of the deep structure than any one surface structure alone, no matter how excellent, could do.

This same Chomsky-Dumézil model can helpfully illustrate the theological method of Rudolf Bultmann, who recognized a variety of "theological thoughts" from the one "kerygma," but had no model to describe what he saw. Faith, for Bultmann, is prior to theology; it is an activity and a relationship of the self to its existence (not, for example, assent to a system of propositions, or a moral virtue); it is a new "self-understanding."

> Faith is something that man does, but it is never something that has been done, never a work that he produces or accomplishes. Rather it is the momentary act in which he lays hold of himself in his God-given freedom. And the man of faith understands himself only in such an act.[19]

The particular activity and relationship that is inherent in the Christian faith Bultmann names the "kerygma. "[20] But that so-far undefined structure, the kerygma, is not directly accesible; we encounter it only in words, that is, only as already formulated in particular theological terminologies. More than one theological conceptual system can be used, but theology cannot be done at all without using some conceptual system: "Every theological exposition of the saving event and of the Christian's existence is constructed with the use of contemporary conceptions. "[21] In terms of the model, faith generates an abstract structure, the kerygma for Christian faith, which is the deep structure. The kerygma must be transformed into surface structures; if the transformations are conceptual systems, the results, which we have in words, are belief structures, or theologies. In addition to those transformations that produce theologies, Bultmann is also concerned with the transformations of the kerygma into living. The task of the believer is "to develop out of his faith an understanding of God, the world, and man in his own concrete situation, "[22] not in just thought.

Bultmann himself concentrated primarily on two sets of theological transformations of the kerygma. One was the mythological conceptual system used so much in the New Testament. Here "myth" is a technical term from the history-of-religions school: language that objectifies the divine in order to present the world from the standpoint of the transcendent, by presenting the transcendent as if it were immanent.[23] The problem that contemporary people face in understanding the New Testament is not that they cannot believe myths; the problem is that unless they can "speak" mythology-- unless they know (consciously or unconsciously) the transformations involved--they will inevitably misunderstand the New Testament.

Mythological conceptual systems are not the only possible transformations. For example, another group, much used in theological work of the past, might be called "idealistic." Bultmann's program (usually labeled "demythologizing, " a term he himself did not choose) intended to analyze the mythological conceptual systems used in the New Testament expressions of the kerygma, to "de-transform" them and then "re-transform" them by means of some other conceptual system which can be better understood today. Bultmann himself thought that the existential-analytic conceptual system of Heidegger was the best candidate for an adequate conceptual system which could be understood today. Thus

his aim was not to state the "pure" kerygma, for example,
by removing the mythological elements to reveal an uninterpreted core. Rather, instead of being uncovered, the kerygma
was to be <u>translated</u>. This Chomsky-Dumézil-Bultmann understanding is generalized in this diagram:[24]

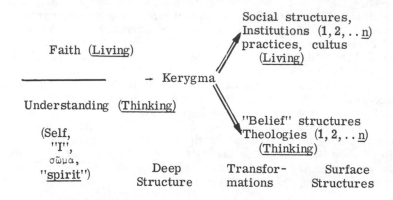

The Transformations are diverse, with differences in time,
cultures, conceptualities, etc., all influencing the particular
Transformation (T) used; hence many Transformations may
be authentic ways of producing a Surface Structure. Some
Transformations may be mythological (such as T_1, T_2,
...T_9), while others may utilize other frameworks (e.g.,
T_{41} through T_{49} might be various Idealist philosophies).
There will be correspondingly diverse Theologies (such as
Theology$_1$, Theology$_2$, ... Theology$_{49}$, etc.) So also with
the diverse institutional forms and structures and practices
which are produced.

As with all translations, theology even if well done
can never be stated once and for all; as situations change,
so must theological statements, in order to be faithful translations of the kerygma. Bultmann's work describes the "theology" of the New Testament in terms of the "theologies" of
the earliest church, of the non-Pauline Hellenistic church,
of Paul, of John and his school, and of the "ancient catholic
church."[25] In each section Bultmann discusses not only the
theologies--the linguistic structures--but also, briefly, the
various developments and changes in the cultus and in the
ecclesiastical and institutional structures. Thus the New
Testament itself presents a picture of a plurality of surface

structures, both belief structures and institutional structures.
Bultmann does not think that all the surface structures in the
New Testament are equally adequate; for example, he remarks, "It cannot be denied that in Col[ossians] and Eph[esians]
there is a certain doctrinairism and moralization in their understanding of salvation. The nature and origin of sin are
not grasped with such depth as in Paul and John. "[26] And
his opinion of parts of Revelation is that they are based on
a different kerygma altogether: Revelation is, at best, a
"weakly Christianized Judaism. "[27] Bultmann sums up the
situation with regard to New Testament theology:

> Unity of doctrine was assured by the canon....
> But that means this unity is only a relative one.
> For in point of fact, the canon reflects a multipli-
> city of conceptions of Christian faith.... Hence,
> its inner unity becomes a question. At any rate,
> such inner unity as is there does not appear with
> the unanimity of dogmatically formulated proposi-
> tions. Beside the synoptics, which even among
> themselves exhibit differences, stands John, and
> beside the Gospels as a whole stands Paul! On one
> side of Paul stands Hebrews, on the other James!
> These variations were not necessarily felt as oppo-
> sites.... But in the course of history these dif-
> ferences inevitably worked out as opposites, and
> when it finally came about that the various Chris-
> tian confessions and sects all appeal for authority
> to the canon, that is possible only because in each
> of them one of the various motifs contained in the
> canonical writings has become the dominant one.[28]

Canonization of this diversity implies that each surface structure, considered alone, is a distortion of the kerygma. All
of them together are needed to give a fuller understanding.

Theological Pluralism

For most of the history of the Christian Church there
has been a picture--in theory, at least--of a uniformity of
theological statements, or doctrines, called "orthodoxy," oper-
ating uniformly within the church. Outside the church, perhaps, there might be some alternate formulations, called
"heresies," always incorrect. It was usually further assumed
that all the writings in the Bible, both Old Testament and New
Testament, were the same as the established orthodoxy. Serious

and systematic questioning of this picture began at the time
of the Enlightenment, with the gradual development of new
methods of investigation. Gradually it became clear that
there were great differences in both approaches and results
in the Scriptural materials and in Christian doctrines over
the centuries. The diversity became more and more apparent as first the Old Testament, then the New Testament, then
church history were investigated using the new methods. Until then the unity of the materials had not been called into
question. But when there was no longer an obvious uniformity, in what sense--if any--was there a unity of the materials?
Various suggestions have been made, none very convincing,
and in some cases a negative answer was given--there is no
unity of Scripture. It may be the case that one difficulty has
been the lack of an adequate model for understanding unity
in diversity. We are now in a position to show how Chomsky's model of language, when extended to belief structures
and theological systems as described in the previous section,
can make sense of the enormous diversity that appears in the
Old Testament, the New Testament, and early Christianity.

Old Testament Theology

When the term "Biblical theology" first appeared in
1629 it named a process of listing Biblical "proof texts" for
the doctrines of Protestant Orthodoxy. [29]   Pietistic use of the
Bible moved "Biblical theology" into opposition to orthodox
doctrine; it was no longer completely subservient to dogmatics but was moving toward becoming a foundation for dogmatics. But the turning point was the rationalism and the developing historical consciousness of the Enlightenment, when
scholars began to study the Bible as they would study any
other ancient literary work, using the gradually developing
historical-critical method. At first the goal was still correct theological doctrine, but now based on historical and
critical exegesis of the Scripture. A significant early effort
of this sort was Gotthilf Traugott Zachariä's 1771-75 work,
Biblische Theologie oder Untersuchung des biblischen Grun-
des der vornehmsten theologischen Lehren, which assumed
that "each book of Scripture has its own time, place, and
intention. "[30]   The independence of "Biblical theology" and
dogmatic theology was expressed by Johann Philipp Gabler
in his inaugural lecture at the University of Altdorf on 30
March 1787:

Biblical theology possesses a historical character,

transmitting what the sacred writers thought about divine matters; dogmatic theology, on the contrary, possesses a didactic character, teaching what a particular theologian philosophizes about divine matters in accordance to his ability, time, age, place, sect or school, and other similar things.[31]

To Gabler there were three things of utmost importance for Biblical theology: first, the Biblical writers must be studied without any idea of divine inspiration that comes between them and the text they produced; second, each individual writer's concepts and ideas must be carefully distinguished and compared with those of the other writers; and third, the ideas presented in the Bible must be placed in their proper historical period and further distinguished as to whether they are valid for modern times or not. Gabler also called for separate treatment of Old Testament theology and New Testament theology.

The first to do this, and the first to realize "the goal of a strictly historical Biblical theology,"[32] was Georg Lorenz Bauer. His Theologie des Alten Testaments was published in 1796 and Biblische Theologie des Neuen Testaments in 1800-02. Although the structure of his Old Testament work shows some dependence on dogmatics--its three parts are theology, anthropology, and Christology--he consistently applied the historical-critical method and showed clearly the diversity of the contents of the Old Testament.

In the nineteenth century the ideas of evolution and of what became the "Religionsgeschichtliche Schule" were applied to the study of the Old Testament, sometimes in combination with a Hegelian point of view. In this way the diversity of the Old Testament was explained as manifestations of various evolutionary stages in the move toward universal or absolute religion (usually Christianity--or at least, ethical monotheism). Gottlob Ph. Chr. Kaiser's Die biblische Theologie (1813-21) was the first to use the history-of-religions method; W. M. L. de Wette's Biblische Dogmatik applied Kantian philosophy and found a "genetic development" of religion from "Hebraism via Judaism to Christianity"; Wilhelm Vatke, in Die biblische Theologie. Die Religion des Alten Testaments (1835), pictured a Hegelian thesis, antithesis, and synthesis in nature religion, Hebrew religion, and Christianity.[33] Even the scholarly conservative reaction against the historical-critical method in the nineteenth century usually acknowledged an "organic process of development":

the "salvation-history school" saw each book of the Bible as
fitting into a linear sequence of history leading up to Jesus
Christ. [34]

The last quarter of the nineteenth century was dominated by the religionsgeschichtlich approach, beginning with
the publication in 1878 of Prolegomena to the History of Israel, by Julius Wellhausen. Wellhausen and his followers
presented a history of Israelite religion using the new dating
of Old Testament materials that was the result of their liter-
acy criticism. Later representatives, such as H. Gunkel,
H. Gressmann, and W. Bousset, expanded the method to study
Israelite religion in its relation to surrounding religions.
According to Hasel, Old Testament theology was no longer
practiced during this period, although the phrase "Old Testament Theology" was "misused" as the title of many books.

> The full-fledged historicism of the "history-of re-
> ligions" approach had led to the final destruction
> of the unity of the OT, which was reduced to a
> collection of materials from detached periods and
> consisted simply of Israelite reflections of as many
> different pagan religions. [35]

It is not clear that that remark is fair to the nineteenth-century versions of the history-of-religions approach, because
many of them did see a real unity in an evolutionary process
from, say, animism to ethical monotheism. But the twentieth
century--that is, post World War I--was less certain about
humanity's upward progress. Looking at the Old Testament
with twentieth-century eyes, many scholars were convinced
that indeed there was no overarching unity, even in evolutionary terms; that the Wisdom literature, to take one example, did not fit neatly into the animism-to-ethical monotheism scheme. At this point Hasel's remark may be appropriate. At the extreme some scholars did take the Old Testament to be irreconcilably diverse, exhibiting the "religions
of Israel," one after another, without any evolutionary goal. [36]

The rise of dialectical theology after World War I allowed an alternative--if not an antimethod--to the history-of-
religions approach.

> To dialectical theology, the religio-historical ap-
> proach was incidental, peripheral, and above all
> untheological.... [Dialectical theology] supplemented
> and corrected the theology that preceded it, but no

postulate of dogmatic theology can explain away the religio-historical data pointed out by the earlier theology. [37]

From the 1930s on most Old Testament scholars have accepted Old Testament theology as a historical discipline in one way or another.

Beginning with Walther Eichrodt in the 1930s there was an attempt to find the unity of the Old Testament without denying the diversity of its materials by looking for a unifying concept or central principle. [38] Eichrodt found this unifying symbol in the idea of covenant, which enables us "to understand the realm of OT belief in its structural unity ... [and] to illuminate its profoundest meaning."[39]

> The concept of the covenant was given this central position in the religious thinking of the OT so that, by working outward from it, the structural unity of the OT message might be made more readily visible. [40]

The idea of covenant is not a doctrine but "the characteristic description of a living process, which was begun at a particular time and at a particular place, in order to reveal a divine reality unique in the whole history of religion."[41] Although Eichrodt sees the covenant as part of a "living process" and allows for historical development, it has since been recognized that no single concept, important though it may be, can include all the variety of Old Testament thoughts. In the case of the covenant concept the Old Testament presents many covenants--e.g., with Abraham, with Moses, with David-- with conflicting features. Further, there seem to be sections of the Old Testament that have nothing at all to do with covenant. Gerhard von Rad asks, "What is there in common between the royal theology and this covenant theology? The king was not an organ of the covenant."[42] Other suggestions for a unifying Old Testament concept were made and eventually dismissed on similar grounds: E. Sellin's holiness of God, Ludwig Köhler's God as the Lord, Hans Wildberger's Israel's election as the people of God, Horst Seebass's rulership of God, Günther Klein's kingdom of God, Georg Fohrer's dual concept the rule of God and the communion between God and humanity, and Th. C. Vriegen's communion. [43]

A new approach came from Gerhard von Rad, who explicitly rejects a "center" of Old Testament theology in the above sense.   It is important and necessary, he says, to study the various Old Testament concepts and their development.   But they cannot be constitutive elements of an Old Testament theology.

> Investigation of such concepts might laboriously produce an overall idea within which the greatest possible number of separate occurrences of them could be included.   Yet, this investigation can only arrive at such a complex of ideas by way of generalisation and abstraction.

But Old Testament theology comes from the continual tension between the various quite definite promises made in Israel's history and the particular quite definite fulfillment that Israel expected in each successive generation.   Thus one should have "no illusions about the limits of such necessarily generalised and abstract investigations of concepts. "[44]

In one sense von Rad can say that the "starting point" and the "center" of Old Testament theology is "Jahweh's action in revelation. "[45]   But that is not a "unifying concept. " "Of course, it can be said that Jahweh is the focal point of the Old Testament.   This is, however, simply the beginning of the whole question: what kind of a Jahweh is he? "   A concept is "too rigid to disclose much of the way in which Jahweh actually revealed himself to his chosen people and was present with them. "[46]   By paying attention to what Israel actually said about Jahweh's action--the subject-matter of Old Testament theology, according to von Rad[47] --the investigator finds that they all have a confessional aspect.   Von Rad calls this their "kerygmatic aspect" or "kerygmatic intention. "[48]   This does not minimize the diversity of the Old Testament elements.   Von Rad points out that there are only a limited number of "great saving appointments, " or base of salvation-- e.g. , the covenant with the patriarchs, or the Sinai covenant-- but each time Israel went back to them she reinterpreted them differently, often violently, both in terms of specific contents and in terms of the expected future. [49]   This "kerygmatic intention" is indeed a unity, although more of form than of content. Von Rad says that oversimplification of the unity--finding it in something external to the Old Testament, such as in a religious or a philosophical concept--is a great danger.

> The most urgent task to-day, as it seems to me, is that of avoiding all conceptions of unity which are not fully authenticated by the material itself.

This appears to me to be the surest way towards a better understanding of what was characteristic of ancient Israel's experience with God. [50]

Hasel accuses von Rad of having a "secret center" of Old Testament theology after all, in spite of von Rad's denial of the possibility of any such center. [51]   Others--for example, Walter Eichrodt--accuse him of having no unity at all.   Both reactions are understandable, if incorrect, because von Rad treated the unity of Old Testament theology as located in the "kerygmatic intent" underlying the materials; it is not in the materials themselves as they are usually studied.   Von Rad did not himself have a way to exhibit how this "kerygmatic intent" could hold together the diversity of the Old Testament, especially since he was concerned to be fair to the diversity and represent it adequately.   Since he sees in the Old Testament "the ceaseless saving movement of promise and fulfilment, then it becomes apparent how the expectations it contains fan out ever wider, then it is no self-contained entity, then it is absolutely open." [52]

Von Rad supplied the raw materials for understanding the Old Testament's unity in diversity, but he had no theory to explain it.   The Chomsky-Dumézil model may provide one. The various traditions and documents in the Old Testament are the diverse surface structures, transformed from one common deep structure, the "kerygmatic intent," in von Rad's terminology: Israel consistently describing herself as standing between God's past promise and his future fulfillment of it.   This "self-understanding," von Rad suggests, is constant.   But which promise is being considered out of a finite lexicon (the covenant with the patriarchs, etc) and which transformations it undergoes are dependent on the situation, and indeed vary with each new generation, producing a new and different surface structure for almost every new occasion. In contrast, the attempts to find a conceptual unity in the Old Testament's diversity were a Structuralist approach, almost an "immediate constituent analysis," saying, in effect, that "covenant" (to take Eichrodt's concept) is an immediate constituent of every tradition in the Old Testament.   That has proved to be as inadequate in Old Testament theology as in language; the diversity was simply too great.   Von Rad recognized the diversity and identified the underlying kerygmatic unity.   What remains to be done to complete von Rad's work is to identify the transformational rules and structures that bring about the diverse surface structures from the one deep structure.

New Testament Theology

New Testament theology, like Old Testament theology, began as the stating of right doctrine. It went through the same stages as Old Testament theology--though generally a little later in any given case--and, until the end of the nineteenth century, found largely a systematic unity in the New Testament, rather than much diversity. There were, of course, exceptions; Martin Luther, for example, recognized loudly a difference between James on the one hand and the epistles of Paul on the other. It is understandable that the New Testament documents presented a picture of more apparent unity than the Old Testament documents; the New Testament documents were written within little more than a century, while the Old Testament represents about a millennium. But by the end of the nineteenth century the history-of-religions school was recognizing an evolutionary history and unity in the New Testament materials, analogous to their results for the Old Testament.[53] This began with William Wrede's Über Aufgabe und Methode der sogenannten neutestamentlichen Theologie in 1897. Heinrich Weinel and Julius Kraft presented other views of the religion of Jesus and the New Testament in books with "New Testament Theology" in their titles,[54] and Wilhelm Bousset's Kyrios Christos (1913) presented yet another view. Johannes Weiss's Die Predigt Jesu vom Reiche Gottes, 1892,[55] proved the importance of apocalyptic eschatology for the New Testament. At the same time more conservative scholars, more or less influenced by the history-of-religions school, continued to find a New Testament unity in doctrinal concepts. Both strands continued into the twentieth century and still exist today.

In his Theology of the New Testament Rudolf Bultmann pointed out two ways to treat the "theological thoughts" of the New Testament: as a system of dogmatics (a systematically ordered unity), or as a variety of writings, each individual, but all a part of a historical continuity. He takes the second approach, continuity (but not evolution):

> By this choice the opinion is expressed that there
> can be no normative Christian dogmatics, in other
> words, that it is not possible to accomplish the
> theological task once for all--the task which con-
> sists of unfolding that understanding of God, and
> hence of the world and man, which arises from
> faith, for this task permits only ever-repeated
> solutions, or attempts at solutions, each in its

particular historical situation. Theology's continuity through the centuries consists not in hold-
ing fast to once formulated propositions but in the
constant vitality with which faith, fed by its origin,
understandingly masters its constantly new historical situation. [56]

This understanding of theology applies to the New Testament
period as well as to modern times; the New Testament materials must also be understood for their diversity, as each
work struggles with its particular historical situation. Bultmann recognized a great diversity in the New Testament; he
also found a unity, not in their content or their evolution,
but in the common kerygma, the "understanding which is inherent in faith."[57] For him each manifestation of the kerygma is shaped by the particular circumstances under which it
is called forth; each manifestation is incomplete, and the
"incompleteness has its cause in the inexhaustibility of believing comprehension, which must ever actualize itself anew."[58]
The particular New Testament actualizations that Bultmann
identifies and considers make up the parts of his Theology
of the New Testament.[59]

Since Bultmann's work the picture he presented has
been carried dramatically further by younger scholars in the
1950s and 1960s who have shown a much greater diversity
of viewpoints than was pictured by Bultmann, diversity present probably from the very beginning of Christianity, and
certainly within the lifetime of Paul. For example, Corinth
was apparently a hotbed of diversity; Paul's opponents in I
Corinthians were investigated by Ulrich Wilckens and those
in II Corinthians (a different group) by Dieter Georgi; Walther Schmithals also dealt with the situation in Corinth.[60]
The discipline of redaction criticism developed and recognized that there were New Testament theologians of great
originality and independence between Paul and John; at least
three of them were the synoptic evangelists.[61] Work on
Mark's theology has been done by, among others, Edward
C. Hobbs, Willi Marxsen, Philipp Vielhauer, and T. J. Weeden.[62] (The recognition of an individual point of view for
the Gospel of Mark fulfills an unconscious prophecy of Albert Schweitzer, who complained that William Wrede described Mark as a writer whose "treatment of the history
scarcely differs from that of the fourth Evangelist."[63]) A
representative work on Matthew using the new approach was
done by G. Bornkamm, G. Barth, and H. J. Held, and Hans
Conzelmann did the same for Luke.[64] That John was an in-

dependent theologian has been recognized for a long time; Bultmann himself produced a significant work on John, and the study of John and the Johannine literature has been continued by many younger scholars.[65] All of these studies and many others like them have shown that the New Testament is much more diverse than was thought even twenty years ago. And thus the problem of its unity has been rendered even more acute.

No one since Bultmann has offered so comprehensive an attempt to deal with the problem of the unity of the New Testament. However, some articles have appeared. In "The Problem of a New Testament Theology" Herbert Braun links the diversities and contradictions in the New Testament to the deeper problem of New Testament (and modern) language about God.[66] Another article with the same title, "The Problem of a New Testament Theology" by Ernst Käsemann,[67] describes what it considers the current impasse and proposes seven theses to further the discussion of how New Testament theology can be given a meaningful structure. Käsemann does not expect a quick solution; he ends his article, "How these theses are to serve as a basis for the actual working out of a New Testament theology remains a problem which cannot be solved in advance. No one can accomplish everything he wants to have done."[68]

In New Testament theology textbooks only two that have come out since Bultmann's are comparable to it. One is the modestly titled An Outline of the Theology of the New Testament, by Hans Conzelmann; the other is Werner Georg Kümmel's The Theology of the New Testament According to Its Major Witnesses: Jesus--Paul--John.[69] A comparison of the two with each other and with Bultmann may illuminate the current difficulties in New Testament theology.

Conzelmann praises Bultmann's work highly for its comprehensiveness and for the way in which "he has been able to embrace both the unity in the New Testament and the multiplicity of approaches, types, outlines, beginnings of systems, which it contains." However, there are two areas in which Bultmann needs updating. One is the result of redaction criticism: the recognition of the synoptic evangelists as theologians in their own right. Conzelmann continues:

> The work of the last two decades has brought out the historical differences even more strongly.
> Among other things, the theology of the individual

authors of the synoptic gospels has become a much-
ploughed field.   This has given rise to the impres-
sion ... that the New Testament tends to break up
into a more or less fortuitous accumulation of "conceptions, " types or "theologies. "[70]

Another reason for the updating is that Bultmann's account
now suffers from a change in perspectives and terminology
that has taken place since he wrote, making it easy to misunderstand Bultmann's interpretaion as psychologistic or pietistic.   Conzelmann agrees with Bultmann that at least part
of the task of New Testament theology is "to provide a positive account of the self-understanding posed by faith";[71] but
Bultmann's own version is slightly out-of-date, and the time
has come for a somewhat new translation--a very Bultmann-
ian position!

To deal with the synoptic evangelists Conzelman adds a
new section, "The Synoptic Kerygma, " to Bultmann's pattern.
However, despite his good intentions, most of the section is the
equivalent of Bultmann's section on the proclamation of Jesus;
Conzelmann anaylzes the synoptic material to arrive at a reconstruction of Jesus's teaching.   Still, the last chapter--
eleven pages out of the fifty-five page section--does deal with
the theology of the three synoptic gospels.   Since Conzelmann
had already done major work on Luke's individual approach, the
shortness of that chapter was certainly not because of ignorance.

To deal with the unity of the New Testament Conzelmann says that he regards New Testament theology as

an exegesis of the original texts of the faith, the
oldest formulations of the creed.   An attempt is
made here to set out the theology of the New Testament in accordance with the present state of the
history of the tradition and thus to provide the
reader with a unitary perspective for exploiting
this discipline.   Such an arrangement may perhaps
help to show a way beyond the alternatives "unity
or multiplicity, " ... so that the multiplicity can
be seen to be a mark of the content, while the
unity is a historical one. [72]

For Conzelmann another expression of the unity is the creed,
which apparently has many formulations (some early versions
of which are in the New Testament).   Although Conzelmann
does not spell it out, it may be a functional equivalent of Bultmann's kerygma.

Conzelmann may not be a great step beyond Bultmann. But in contrast, Kümmel seems to be a step backward. As his subtitle makes clear, he confines himself to the "major witnesses": Jesus, Paul, John. He admits that limiting himself to these three "could appear arbitrary, and it in no way proceeds from the conviction that the other writings of the New Testament are unimportant or at least of less value." But study of the three major witnesses will produce "a clear and adequate picture of the central proclamation of the New Testament, to which then the message of the remaining writings can be related."[73] (Presumably the "remaining writings" include the synoptic writers, but this is not specifically stated.) The order of procedure must first be to study the individual writings in their own right, without trying to put them into a preconceived framework.

> The task of a theology of the New Testament can in no case consist primarily in presenting the views of the New Testament comprehensively as a whole. For in such a procedure one of two things would unavoidably occur: either the views of the individual writings or groups of writings are forcibly fitted together into a median outlook, or divergent ideas are sacrificed to the dominant ones. The task of a theology of the New Testament can only consist in first allowing the individual writings or groups of writings to speak for themselves, and only then to ask about the unity which is shown therein, or else to affirm a diversity which cannot be eliminated.[74]

Kümmel does, in this section, anticipate his final answer to the question by speaking of the "central proclamation" of the New Testament, which manifests itself in various forms.[75] But at the end, after his investigation of his "three major witnesses," he concludes that the "heart of the New Testament" is the

> twofold message, that God has caused his salvation promised for the end of the world to begin in Jesus Christ, and that in this Christ event God has encountered us and intends to encounter us as the Father who seeks to rescue us from imprisonment in the world and to make us free for active love.[76]

Kümmel seems to have arrived at this formulation by finding a sort of highest common factor in his three major witnesses,

but it seems that he has not avoided the danger that he himself pointed out earlier, that of sacrificing the divergent ideas.
His formula seems too weak to include the repentance usually
considered an important part of Jesus's message, for example. The problem is that Kümmel's particular formulation is as inadequate as all other attempts to find the unity
of the New Testament in a particular doctrine or message
of "divine truth."[77]   In this also he has moved a step backward.

If Conzelmann's approach is a variant on Bultmann's,
as he himself implies, then the contrast of method between
Bultmann/Conzelmann and Kümmel and the inadequacy of
Kümmel's approach can be illuminated by the Transformational-Generative analysis presented here. The details of
a T-G analysis of Bultmann were given above;[78] briefly, he
finds the unity of the New Testament in the kerygma, the
deep structure, which never appears in itself but always
transformed into a variety of "theological thoughts"--surface
structures. Possible transformational systems (among others)
are those of mythology (used in the New Testament) and existentialism (used by Bultmann). These systems have been
analyzed in some detail, although not, of course, as transformational systems, by Bultmann and Heidegger in particular. Bultmann is completely open about what he is doing
and how he is doing it. But his lack of an appropriate model
for his approach obscured investigation of the adequacy of
his "translation," leaving him more open to charges of dis-
torting the Christian faith than perhaps would have been the
case if he had been able to demonstrate the "mechanisms"
involved--that is, if the transformational rules involved in
both the New Testament theologies and in Bultmann's own
transformation of the kerygma had been made explicit. This
has not yet been done.

In the case of Kümmel his formulation of the "heart
of the New Testament" is at best one surface structure formulation of the Christian deep structure. The fact that he
arrived at his particular formulation apparently by a completely surface-structure procedure does not seem promising
for its adequacy as even one among many alternate possible
surface structures. However, the real question is whether
the formulation is a possible (in this case, unconscious) transformation of the kerygma, and to answer that, the transformations involved have to be identified.

To sum up, investigations over the past few centuries

and increasingly within the past few decades have shown the diverse points of view represented in the New Testament. During most of this period attempts have been made to identify a unity in the New Testament, often by explicitly or implicitly denying that the pluralism is real. Chomsky's work, as supplemented by Dumézil and as exhibited by Bultmann, may provide a way out of the apparent impasse. What remains to be done is to carry out the program! Specifically, the transformational system or systems used by each writer or group need to be identified, and, concurrently, the phrase structures and thematic relations possible in the kerygma. In this approach the plurality of the surface structures is an advantage rather than the opposite; each surface structure emphasizes some aspects of the deep structure and obscures others. Dealing with a number of surface structures, then, allows for a richer understanding of the deep structure.

It might happen that some particular writer or group of writers in the New Testament might turn out to be really different from the others, might really be transformed from a different kerygma, even though possibly using some identical transformations. That is still an open question. At the moment there is no particular reason to think that that will happen, although it might be remembered that the canon of Scripture is not entirely uniform among Christian churches-- Eastern Orthodox churches, for example, do not use readings from Revelation. In any case the surface-structure "contradictions" noticed now may be the result of the transformational options chosen by each New Testament writer; they might also appear as a result of surface-structure-related aspects of meaning. It seems likely that there is indeed a unity in the canonical New Testament at the deep-structure level.

One other advantage of this model for Biblical theology can be mentioned. The kerygma, since it is deep structure, never appears "pure" but always in some linguistic form. This is as true of the Biblical scholar's attempts to state it as it is of the statements of the New Testament writers the scholar is investigating. Therefore investigators must also choose a transformational system to use for their statements of the kerygma. Although the past is littered with scholars who have applied some particular method to everyone they deal with except themselves, and scholars using a T-G method may be no exception, it is possible that scholars using this method would be aware that the process applies to themselves also. Therefore, they might not choose their

own transformational system unconsciously or at random, but
with some effort to pick one that would seem useful or appropriate to their audience. Ideally such a transformational
system would be, or be made, explicit, so the scholars' results could be more clearly evaluated. When this is done
there is yet another desirable result: a natural connection
between two often separate disciplines, Biblical theology and
constructive theology.

Early Christianity

The problem of pluralism and unity appears in the
study of the Christian church in its first few centuries, where
a diversity of belief and doctrines is exhibited. Until quite
recently, that pluralism was usually understood as a matter
of an original, more or less uniform orthodoxy, the "Great
Church," contrasted with later and derivative, and even par-
asitic, breakaway movements, the heresies. This understanding was described in its most simplistic form as follows:[79]

(1) Jesus reveals the pure doctrine to his apostles,
     partly before his death, and partly in the forty
     days before his ascension.

(2) After Jesus' final departure, the apostles ap-
     portion the world among themselves, and each
     takes the unadulterated gospel to the land which
     has been allotted him.

(3) Even after the death of the disciples the gos-
     pel branches out further. But now obstacles
     to it spring up within Christianity itself. The
     devil cannot resist sowing weeds in the divine
     wheatfield--and he is successful at it. True
     Christians blinded by him abandon the pure
     doctrine. This development takes place in the
     following sequence: unbelief, right belief,
     wrong belief. . . .

(4) Of course, right belief is invincible. In spite
     of all the efforts of Satan and his instruments,
     it repels unbelief and false belief, and extends
     its victorious sway even further.

In this picture, of course, heretics are always people
who really know better but who leave the church for evil motives. Mani, for example, was said to have left the church
because his students were not appreciated. A fit of pique
over failure to become bishop is charged to Bardesanes, Val-

entinus, and Marcion. [80] Similar stories have been told down
the centuries, for example about Mohammed and Luther.

    With the rise of modern scholarship and historical so-
phistication this picture was modified somewhat, usually in
the direction of an evolutionary understanding. It was recognized that, for example, Jesus did not instruct the apostles
in every tenet of Christian belief, but that the body of Christian doctrine developed gradually over the centuries, at least
partly in response to the situations the Church encountered.
Sometimes this development was seen as merely making explicit what was always present in Christian doctrine, but previously implicit; sometimes it was seen as real change and
newness, altering or increasing previous doctrine. The apos-
tolic geography was questioned, and also the apostles' role
as protectors of the pure faith. The assumption that all
heresies were caused by the frustrated ambition or other
shoddy motives of their founders was dropped, and some
heretics, at least, were "rehabilitated" as people who had
sincerely tried to interpret Christian belief in ways that were
appropriate or at least reasonable for their time but were
rendered obsolete by the subsequent development of Christianity in other directions. Yet even this greatly modified view
of early Christianity pictured a unitary, although developing,
original orthodoxy, with heresies growing out of the primary
orthodoxy. The sequence is still unbelief, right belief, wrong
belief.

    Walter Bauer questioned this picture at length in his
book Orthodoxy and Heresy in Earliest Christianity. After
examining the history of Christianity in several places in the
ancient world he concluded that the type of Christianity that
was subsequently called orthodoxy was originally largely limited to the city of Rome. Other versions of Christianity were
original elsewhere and flourished to such an extent that they
were "Christianity" in those places. Those few sympathetic
to Roman-type Christianity in those other regions had to be
identified by other names--"Palûtians," for example, in
Edessa. [81] By various means, using its influence and power
as the chief city of the Roman empire, Rome extended its
influence eastward, first to Corinth (by about A.D. 100), then
to Antioch, and after a century or more, to Alexandria.
(The process is analogous to the way in which a "language"
comes to be distinguished from a "dialect" in the pejorative
sense--a "language" is the dialect of a center of power.)
Rome's means of influence almost certainly included finan-
cial support for those who agreed with her, enabling them,

for example, to buy out Christian slaves and prisoners. [82]
In all of this Rome truly believed herself to be acting in the
service of truth and for the best motives.

Rome's techniques also included the rewriting of history along the lines of the "ecclesiastical picture" described
above, showing that the "winning side" was really the original side. One method in the rewriting was to establish a
connection with an apostle, one of the twelve who had been
with Jesus. Rome originally appealed to Peter and Paul,
although Paul was dropped about the end of the second century, when controversy made appeal to a single (and later,
monarchical) episcopal founder more desirable--and Peter's
relationship with Jesus was clearer than Paul's. Under Roman pressure Peter emerged as the founder of the church
in Corinth and in Antioch, and Mark (taken to be Peter's
"son and interpreter") in Alexandria. [83] Rome also gradually
imposed an ecclesiastical structure on the churches she took
under her/wing; her advantages here were the Roman genius
for organization and the diffusiveness of most other types of
Christianity, making it hard for any one of them to structure
itself, let alone form common cause with other groups against
Rome.

> It was only natural that the compact ecclesiastical
> outlook with its concentrated energy would more and
> more draw to itself the great mass of those who
> at first, unclear and undecided, had stood in the
> middle resigned to a general sort of Christianity,
> and who under different circumstances could even
> have turned in the opposite direction. [84]

Thus came about the "Great Church."

In the decades since the original publication of Bauer's
work many of the details of Bauer's reconstruction of the original churches have been shown to be incorrect. However,
his main thesis has not been disproved, and has proved useful in many other areas of investigation. [85] To summarize,
Bauer suggested that Christianity originally manifested itself
in a variety of ways, no one of which was "orthodoxy." But
the variety of Christianity in Rome was in a position to exercise political, social, and economic power over the other
varieties and used this power to dominate them, either ex-
terminating them or driving them out of the "Great Church."
It then read its victorious situation back into the past, inter-
preting history to show itself as the original form of Christi-

anity and the direct heir and successor of Jesus. In other
words, "orthodoxy" is the Christianity of the winner--and
the victory was won by political, social, and economic means,
not by theological continuity or primitivity.

Thus here again the problem of the unity of Christianity arises. Bauer himself did not address this question; he
did not attempt to show what, if anything, holds together these
diverse manifestations all calling themselves Christianity and
often denying the name to those of a different type. It would
be difficult or impossible to find anything major that all or
even most of them had in common: they had different doctrines, different ecclesiastical organizations, even different
Scriptures. Again, the T-G approach provides a model. The
same kerygma may underlie a real pluralism of surface manifestations, even apparently antithetical surface structures.[86]
And, on the other hand, somewhat similar surface structures
could arise from different kerygmas. The transformational
systems would have to be analyzed before judgments about
"orthodoxy" and "heresy" could be made. In any case any
single surface manifestation, no matter what its history, is
clearly not adequate to represent the richness of the kerygma.
The resistance to the idea of original diversity rather than
original orthodoxy is partly due to the fear that it leads to
relativism, to a total absence of distinction among whatever
systems might call themselves Christian--"German Christianity," for example, under Hitler. (Bauer's book, incidentally,
first attracted major attention in Germany after World War
II, when the Church there was faced with a new Donatist controversy between the "Confessional Church" and the "Confess-
ing Church," and the question of the nature of orthodoxy
and its relation to heresy became of great practical importance.) The T-G model, if spelled out, allows for a pluralism of legitimate surface structures of the Christian kerygma,
while providing a means to distinguish these from surface
structures that are transformed from a different kerygma.
Thus there is not one "orthodoxy," but many; yet not everything is orthodox. Bauer showed the genuine variety that was
present in early Christianity; T-G analysis can show the genuine unity.

Religious Pluralism

The rise of the history-of-religions school and the
problems it posed for the study of the Old Testament have
been already discussed. But it created yet another problem

when the religious (as distinguished from the theological) aspect of its discoveries was considered.   The uniqueness of
the Christian religion was called into question as its similarities to other religions began to be known, and it proved fruit-
ful to study Christianity as one example of parallel human
religious manifestations.   Ernst Troeltsch was one who belonged to the history-of-religions school and yet struggled
with the problem it posed to what he called the "absoluteness"
of Christianity.   He pointed out that the uniqueness or absoluteness of Christianity had been thought to be the result of
its unique supernatural origin, and its miracles verified this.
However, once Christianity was seen as a part of the historical context of human life, rather than an exception to it--
especially once it was put into the context of other religions
and religion-like movements--it was impossible to justify re-
taining the Christian claim to uniqueness based on miracles
while at the same time rejecting the similar or identical
claims made by other religions.   The problematic nature of
miracles for the modern mind is not here the point; although
Troeltsch recognizes "the trouble attendant upon every theory
of miracles,"[87] the major difficulty is that there is no prin-
cipled reason--that is, it is dishonest--to pick out Christianity's claims over the identical claims of other religions.   Troeltsch quotes with approval a remark by Kant that if the theologians do not pursue honest investigation, the "freethinkers"
will, and will then "drag the orthodox about anywhere as if
they were children; they may not put up the slightest resistance, for by their own protestation they cannot match themselves against one who possesses such authority."[88]   The
original investigation in Kant's remark was philology, but
Troeltsch applies it to historical study.   A return to a simpler past, when historical investigation did not present a
problem, is impossible and unhistorical, and, since Christianity itself is historical, such a return would be un-Christian.

There was another method to try to maintain the uniqueness of Christianity in the face of the growing body of
knowledge of other religions, and that was the evolutionary
method already discussed in connection with Biblical study.
Christianity was seen as the culmination of a linear evolutionary process that has led from animism to polytheism to
ethical monotheism.   However, this view is not tenable either.
In the first place, there are no genetic connections among
all the world's religions, not even among the world's great
religions.   They stand in a parallel relationship to each other,
not in a "step-by-step-causal" chain.[89]   Further, there are
irreconcilable differences among them, inconsistent with the

idea of a continuous development.   Finally, Christianity itself
is not free of historical conditioning; it does not present an
."unchanging essence"--not even the universal principle of
religion--down through the centuries that can be compared
to those of other religions.   "There is no such thing," inside or outside of Christianity, "as an unchangeably fixed
truth."[90]   Christianity presents

> no historical uniformity, but displays a different
> character in every age, and is, besides, split up
> into many different denominations, hence it can in
> no wise be represented as the finally attained uni-
> ty and explanation of all that has gone before....
> It is rather a particular, independent, historical
> principle, containing, similarly to the other prin-
> ciples, very diverse possibilities and tendencies.[91]

But then the question is whether Christians can go beyond the
diversity that historical investigation shows, the apparent
relativity of all human religions, into a value decision about
a religious norm for their own lives.

The fear of relativism, Troeltsch says, comes partly
from a misunderstanding of what the discipline of history actually is and does, especially its contrast with the natural
sciences.   Following Wilhelm Dilthey, Troeltsch distinguished
between the Naturwissenschaften and the Geisteswissenschaf-
ten, the natural sciences and the other bodies of systematized
knowledge.[92]   The quantitative, generalizing approach--the
"causal-mechanistic" model--is appropriate and successful in
the natural sciences, but if it is applied to the Geisteswissen-
schaften, it causes the loss of what is essential to them, the
"individual and unique."   "Our thinking about causation is too
much under the influence of a naturalistic scholasticism."[93]
However, even if natural-science causality is avoided, there
still seems to be the relativism of the historians' prolifera-
tion of details, apparently for their own sake and all of equal
importance.   Troeltsch admits that this goes on, but it is not
history; " ... it is, rather, clay for the bricks with which
history is made."[94]   Troeltsch is concerned to point out that
genuine historical relativity is not the denial of all value and
meaning in history; it is not the assumption that everything
is as worthwhile as everything else.   He sums up his view
of the historical method:

> The historical method must be conceived in such a
> way that what is relative and individual in history

will come into its own as a factor that dominates
history unconditionally. Yet it must also be con-
ceived in such a way as not to exclude from these
individual and relative phenomena the emergence of
authentic values which, in consequence of their
validity, are directed toward a common goal.[95]

To deal with Christianity according to this historical
method we need to investigate Christianity on its own terms.
We may seek out the "controlling idea of Christianity" and
try "to understand, as far as possible, the development and
continuation of Christianity in view of the content of this idea."
But all metaphors, such as kernel and husk, form and content, abiding truth and temporal-historical conditions, must
be abandoned.[96] The "controlling idea" is not transcendent
or ahistorical but always involved in historically conditioned,
therefore changing, forms. There may be an "essence,"
or better, a "nature" of Christianity, but it is not an unchanging essence. It may be called an "absolute" purpose
or goal that constantly manifests itself anew in varying historical forms in Christianity. It is not found in any abstrac-
tion but only embodied in the positive, historical, religious
manifestations of Christianity. However, the "absolute" goal
is never completely embodied in any particular historical
manifestation, all of which can represent only more or less
of it. Troeltsch thinks that there can be a kind of non-dog-
matic personal conviction that can emerge from open-minded
involvement in comparative religious studies and "absorption
in hypothetically adopted values," a personal conviction that
Christianity is indeed "the highest realm of religious life
and thought that has validity for us."[97] It has, in Troeltsch's
opinion, succeeded best out of all the great religions in synthesizing the separate tendencies and impulses that have arisen in the great world religions. It contains within itself
more possibilities for new syntheses both past and future
than any other; thus its "absoluteness" is "simply the highest
value discernible in history and the certainty of having found"
--not the perfect truth, but--"the way that leads to perfect
truth."[98] This is not meant to remove the historical uniqueness of Christianity.

The universal law of history consists precisely in
this, that ... the Divine Life, within history, constantly manifests itself in always-new and always-
peculiar individualizations--and hence that its tendency is not towards unity or universality at all,
but rather towards the fulfilment of the highest

potentialities of each separate department of life. It is this law which, beyond all else, makes it quite impossible to characterize Christianity as the reconciliation and goal of all the forces of history, or indeed to regard it as anything else than as a historical individuality.[99]

Troeltsch would emphasize this individuality in both past and present forms of Christianity, including denominational forms, although he missed it in the period of Christian origins (as did almost everyone else before Bauer): " ... in our day churches ... no longer need the passionate insistence on conformity which was both possible and necessary in the days of their beginnings."[100] Troeltsch's method

> strives constantly to make the closest possible connection with the living power of historical Christianity. ... But ... it presupposes an individual diversity among the different theologians in a church, and, in so far, it renounces the unyielding power of a dogma to which all alike must be subject. ... It is the duty of the churches, if they are to meet the needs of life itself, to guarantee individual freedom. Hence a dogmatics such as we have indicated can meet the needs of certain believers, while needs of a different type will be met by a different sort of dogmatics.[101]

For Troeltsch the pluralism of contemporary religious expressions was a positive aspect of Christianity, something to be appreciated and affirmed.

The diversity of Christianity that expresses itself in denominational difference has, of course, not usually been appreciated. Members of different groups have engaged in mutual distrust, suspicion, and even excommunication; each group has tended to think that it held to essential Christianity, and that therefore the only possible basis for Christian unity was for every other group to abandon its position and accept the truth. Obviously, ecumenism made little headway under this mentality.

Yet the ecumenical movement has been significant for twentieth-century Christianity; for convenience its beginning may be dated in 1907, when the Graymoor Fathers began what became the Week of Prayer for Christian Unity every year between the Feasts of the Confession of St. Peter and

the Conversion of St. Paul (18-25 January).   The observance
of this week gradually spread.   In the meantime other strands
of cooperative action had been developed and were coming
together; two of the most important were named "Life and
Work" and "Faith and Order."[102]   Several national-level interdenominational organizations concerned with common ethical action and service had been formed in the late nineteenth
and early twentieth centuries, and this led to the first Universal Christian Conference on Life and Work at Stockholm
in 1925.   The second world gathering with the "Life and Work"
theme was the conference on Church, Community, and State
at Oxford in 1937.   (This was timed to meet in sequence
with another 1937 conference, the second one on Faith and
Order, which met at Edinburgh.)   The "Faith and Order"
movement was an attempt to face frankly the theological and
doctrinal differences among the Christian churches that could
often be glossed over in discussions in other areas--ethical
action, for example.   In 1910 the General Convention of the
Episcopal Church in the United States adopted a resolution
urging that a conference be set up "for the consideration of
questions touching Faith and Order and all Christian Com-
munions throughout the world which confess our Lord Jesus
Christ as God and Saviour be asked to unite with us in ar-
ranging for and conducting such a conference."[103]   The first
World Conference on Faith and Order met in Lausanne in
1927.   The second was the 1937 Edinburgh conference already
mentioned.   Both 1937 conferences--Oxford and Edinburgh--
voted to integrate, and a provisional structure for the World
Council of Churches was adopted in Utrecht the following year.
The World Council remained "in process of formation" throughout World War II; its First Assembly was held in Amsterdam
in 1948, when the major Protestant bodies of Europe, America, and the Pacific, and many from Asia and Africa, and
some Orthodox bodies joined on the basis that "the World
Council of Churches is a fellowship of churches which accept
our Lord Jesus Christ as God and Saviour."[104]

The working assumption behind much of the discussion
of these meetings was that most, if not all, of Christian
diversity was caused by a lack of mutual understanding.   If
only the different groups could explain themselves to each
other, they would find that they really have very much in
common.   What they all have in common, then, is essential
Christianity, and is the basis for unity.   What is not common must be optional and nonessential.

As this assumption was put into practice it was dis-

covered to be totally inadequate. Although the various conferences and meetings were able to come up with careful formulations that everyone could accept--such as the "Basis" of
the World Council of Churches, just quoted--they were clearly
not a very useful highest common factor, such as had been
expected to emerge. Some formulations were so vague as
to be open to the charge of meaninglessness; others were
acceptable only because they were capable of being construed
in totally different ways by different groups. And, of course,
few churches agreed in practice that every item that could
not be covered by one of those careful formulations was in-
essential and optional.

The failure of this approach was recognized at the
Third World Conference on Faith and Order held at Lund in
1952. At this point it was clear that the churches were on
the whole understanding each other fairly well, and that there
was no significant highest common factor. They were, to
this approach, irreconcilably diverse. The Final Report
from the Lund Conference says,

> We have seen clearly that we can make no real
> advance toward unity if we only compare our sever-
> al conceptions of the nature of the church and the
> traditions in which they are embodied.... We need,
> therefore, to penetrate behind our divisions to a
> deeper and richer understanding. [105]

However, no one knew how to move forward. Progress toward unity was at a dead end, and it is significant that the
next major conference, the Second World Assembly of the
World Council of Churches at Evanston, Illinois, in 1954,
discussed eschatology as its major topic. [106]

The breakthrough in this impasse came from the Roman Catholic Church. Roman Catholics had taken little official part in the ecumenical movement; the 1928 encyclical of
Pope Pius XI, Mortalium Animos, temporarily closed the
door by stating that Christian unity could be brought about
only "by furthering the return to the one true Church of Christ
of those who are separated from it," adding that all must
believe in "the infallibility of the Roman Pontiff in the sense
of the OEcumenical Vatican Council [I] with the same faith
as they believe in the Incarnation of Our Lord."[107] This
pattern was broken by Pope John XXIII, who was elected in
1958.

John XXIII's real contributions to ecumenism were of
two kinds: his own actions and the works of the Second Vatican Council, which he announced on 25 June 1959. Vatican
II began on 11 October 1962 and met for four sessions, in
the autumns of 1962 through 1965. John XXIII died on 3
June 1963, but his successor, Pope Paul VI, carried on the
Council. The Council included more than two thousand bishops from all over the world, who represented a great diversity and even disagreement of opinion on everything the Council considered. Nevertheless, a strong stand on ecumenism
was taken in the Decree on Ecumenism, whose final form
was approved by a vote of 2,054 to 64 and promulgated by
Paul VI on 21 November 1964. (John XXIII saw the first
version of this Decree and had that version sent around the
world to the Council Fathers a few weeks before he died.)
This document explicitly states that non-Roman Catholic Christians "have a right to be honored by the title of Christian,
and are properly regarded as brothers in the Lord" by Roman Catholics; that "both sides" share the blame for the
church's current divisions; and that non-Roman Catholic
"Churches and Communities, though we believe they suffer
from defects, ... have by no means been deprived of significance and importance in the mystery of salvation."[108] Furthermore, all faithful Roman Catholics should "participate
skillfully in the work of ecumenism."[109] This put the Roman Catholic Church into the heart of the ecumenical movement.

Some of the other documents of Vatican II, although
not dealing specifically with ecumenism, provided a helpful
model for subsequent ecumenical understanding. They recognized the diversity of opinion within the Roman Catholic Church
as represented by the members of the Council and actually
wrote that pluralism into the Constitutions of the Council.
For example, the Dogmatic Constitution on the Church, Lumen Gentium, does not define the church in a hierarchical
or juridical way--say, as a uniform body with everyone and
everything in its divinely appointed place. Rather it presents the meaning of the church in a series of "pastoral,
Christocentric, biblical, historical, and eschatological" images.[110] Furthermore, the responsibility for the work of
the entire church is placed not in an isolated papacy but in
the collegiality of all the bishops--including, of course, the
pope as the head of the College. It is significant that this
document was the most drastically revised of all the Council
documents. The first draft, prepared by the Theological Com-
mission in 1962 before Vatican II's first session, was "an

ominous sample of what has been called the 'siege mentality of pre-conciliar Rome.' "[111] This was rejected by the Council Fathers, and a new document was drafted between the first and the second sessions, and this also was subsequently thoroughly revised, and amended yet again before its final approval (2,151 to 5) on 21 November 1964. The conflict over collegiality was the "most crucial conflict"; its resolution "marked the turning point in the Council's history."[112] The resolution for collegiality was for a kind of pluralism.

Another example is the Pastoral Constitution on the Church in the Modern World, Gaudium et Spes, the longest single document of the Council. It was addressed "not only to the sons of the Church and to all who invoke the name of Christ, but to the whole of humanity."[113] It discusses the relationship of the Church to various elements of the modern world in a way that affirms that positive values are present in many of them, and that real dialog with them is possible. For example (and there are many such examples),

> recent studies and findings of science, history, and philosophy raise new questions which influence life and demand new theological investigations.... Theologians are invited to seek continually for more suitable ways of communicating doctrine to the men of their times. For the deposit of faith or revealed truths are one thing; the manner in which they are formulated without violence to their meaning and significance is another.[114]

Thus the church may enter into real dialog with so-called "secular" manifestations of humanity for the greater enrichment of all. Social and political pluralism are explicitly allowed. "Many different people go to make up the political community, and these can lawfully incline toward diverse ways of doing things."[115] Finally, the conclusion calls for "dialogue between all men," first that we should "foster within the Church herself mutual esteem, reverence, and harmony, through the full recognition of lawful diversity." Others with whom dialog should take place are "those brothers and communities not yet living with us in full communion," "all who acknowledge God," "those who cultivate beautiful qualities of the human spirit, but do not yet acknowledge the Source of these qualities," and "those who oppress the Church."[116]

But even more than the "lawful diversity" embodied in the documents of Vatican II were the actions of John XXIII himself.   One was his 1963 encyclical <u>Pacem in Terris</u>, addressed to "all men of good will." He received and acknowledged the Archbishop of Canterbury, paving the way for his successor, Paul VI, to visit the Patriarch of Constantinople in early 1964.   (On 7 December 1965 the Pope and the Patriarch issued a joint declaration of regret for the past, charity for the present, and hope of reconciliation for the future, and removed their churches' mutual excommunications of each other.)   John XXIII also named five official Roman Catholic observers to the Third Assembly of the World Council of Churches in New Delhi in 1961; since then Roman Catholic representation, one way or another, on the World Council and its organs has been constant.   As part of the preparation for Vatican II John XXIII established a Secretariat for Promoting Christian Unity under Augustin Cardinal Bea to provide a channel for dialog with other churches; he also invited non-Roman Catholic observers to attend the Council, and had them seated in St. Peter's across the aisle from the Cardinals.   In all these actions the Pope recognized the validity of diversity in the Christian Church, even acknowledging the heads of other Christian communities, while as yet there was no "solution" to the religious and theological differences among the churches.   This practical stance towards diversity--the willingness to acknowledge the authenticity and validity of diverse forms of religious life, polity, theology, liturgy, and practices, among others--was what John XXIII embodied, and the Council expressed his position.

This stance of acceptance of pluralism, rather than an insistence on the substitution of a single common factor in place of pluralism, was implicitly accepted by the World Council of Churches and rapidly gained ground within Protestantism.   (The Orthodox, who have tended to think of themselves in territorial terms, have remained aloof.)   Some evidence comes from a study of denominational mergers during this period.   In the United States Lutheran church mergers took place in 1918, 1930, and the early 1940s, leaving three main bodies, the Lutheran Church in America, the Lutheran Church--Missouri Synod, and the American Lutheran Church. Presbyterians merged in 1906 and 1958; Unitarians and Universalists in 1961, and various Methodists in 1939, 1946, and 1968.   Across denominational lines the United Church of Christ came into being in 1957 after mergers of different bodies at different times.   The most famous example of a cross-denominational merger is outside the U.S., the Church of South India, which in 1948 joined former Presbyterians, Congregationalists, Methodists, and Anglicans.

What is interesting is that since Vatican II ended in the mid-sixties, the momentum toward mergers seems to have slackened. As an example, on 4 December 1960 in San Francisco's Grace Cathedral, Eugene Carson Blake, Stated Clerk of the United Presbyterian Church in the U.S.A., preached the sermon "A Proposal Toward the Unity of Christ's Church." Out of this grew the Consultation on Church Unity (COCU), which began work in 1962. It involved nine denominations, but nothing much came of it. It missed the high time of the merging spirit, which seems to have faded not because of antiecumenism but because of a new understanding: mergers and uniformity may not be the solution after all, but rather the appreciation of our differences and the affirmation and valuing of our diversity. One example of this new understanding may be the Graduate Theological Union: it is a union-in-diversity of nine different seminaries (and a few associated centers), not a merger into one interdenominational seminary.

Even when the value of diversity is recognized, there has been no model to explain it except the originally Stoic model of the organism adopted by Paul. The model hinges on the diversity of functions in the body, and there is a tendency for people to identify the functions and then assign the important functions to privileged groups. (For example, Pope Pius XII used the model in <u>Mystici Corporis</u> to say that a body must have a head to direct it, and that head is the pope.) What is needed is a model in which there is no opportunity for invidious comparisons or distinctions among the elements. The Transformational-Generative model avoids that danger.

Much of Christianity, including Roman Catholicism, is now where Troeltsch was at the beginning of the century, with a recognition of historical diversity and an appreciation of present diversity but with no method of distinguishing what Vatican II called "lawful diversity" from possible other systems masquerading as Christian. The T-G model provides a basis for the distinction: any surface structure transformed from the one kerygma, the Christian deep structure, would be a member of the "lawful diversity"; surface structures transformed from other kerygmas would not be, even if they used the same transformations. To paraphrase Troeltsch, a surface structure that suited one person might not suit another; the other might need a different surface structure. Expressions of the diversity inherent in a T-G understanding of Christianity is not a weakening of Christianity but its continual reincarnation into the concrete, historical world--the only place it is accessible to human beings. Speaking of what we have called the surface structure, Troeltsch has the last word: "An unchangeable Christianity would mean the end of Christianity itself. There has never been such an unchangeable Christianity and never can be so long as it belongs genuinely to history."[117]

Notes

[1]Emile Durkheim, The Elementary Forms of the Religious Life, trans. Joseph Ward Swain (New York: Macmillan, Free Press, 1965), p. 22.

[2]This description of Dumézil's thought is taken from C. Scott Littleton, The New Comparative Mythology: An Anthropological Assessment of the Theories of Georges Dumézil, rev. ed. (Berkeley and Los Angeles: University of California Press, 1973). Hereafter called NCM. Dumézil's system is not universally accepted; both the system itself and the details of its application have been criticized by a number of scholars. On the other hand, many scholars support Dumézil vigorously. Littleton remarks that "most of the scholars who have concerned themselves with Dumézil's ideas regarding the nature of I-E myth, society, and ideology fall into one of two broad categories: disciples and critics." There are few neutrals. (NCM, p. 153.) In any case, Dumézil is probably the current leading comparative mythologist.

[3]Georges Dumézil, "La préhistoire indo-iranienne des castes," Journal asiatique 216 (1930): 109-30.

[4]Emile Benveniste, "Les classes sociales dans la tradition avestique," Journal asiatique 221 (1932): 117-34.

[5]C. Scott Littleton, Introduction to Part I of Gods of the Ancient Northmen, by Georges Dumézil, ed. Einar Haugen (Berkeley and Los Angeles: University of California Press, 1973), p. xv.

[6]Georges Dumézil, Les Dieux des Indo-Européens (Paris: Presses Universitaires de France, 1952), p. 7, quoted in NCM, p. 8.

[7]These examples are from NCM, pp. 7-9, 11-12, 71-72.

[8]Introduction to Gods of the Ancient Northmen, p. x,
n. 3.

[9]Ibid., p. xxviii. Note 29 on the same page adds:
"It should be emphasized that Professor Dumézil himself does
not suggest that there is any necessary connection between
the tripartite ideology of the ancient Indo-Europeans and the
widespread tendency among contemporary Indo-European speakers to structure their thinking along tripartite lines. It is
an anthropological implication for which I must take sole responsibility."

[10]NCM, p. 216.

[11]Benjamin Lee Whorf, Language, Thought and Reality,
ed. John B. Carroll (Cambridge, Mass.: MIT Press, 1956).

[12]Introduction to Gods of the Ancient Northmen, p. xvii;
NCM, p. 232.

[13]Actually, if Dumézil's pattern applies, it is probably
Son, Father, Spirit. These examples are from NCM, pp.
231-32.

[14]Littleton comments: "Dumézil has recently suggested
(personal communication) that the principal question ... is
whether the tripartite social organization of Medieval Europe
survives primarily from the Celtic or the Germanic variant
of the common Indo-European structure." Introduction to
Gods of the Ancient Northmen, p. xviii, n. 27.

[15]For example, Claude Lévi-Strauss, "Social Structure,"
in Anthropology Today, ed. A. L. Kroeber (Chicago: University of Chicago Press, 1953), p. 535, and Le cru et le cuit
(Paris: Plon, 1964), pp. 23, 300, both quoted in NCM, p.
185.

[16]NCM, pp. 5-6, 62.

[17]Professor Edward C. Hobbs, on his sabbatical leave
in 1975-76, worked out the following T-G analysis of Dumézil and first presented it to a GTU doctoral seminar
(PH 618, Transformational-Generative Hermeneutics) during
Fall Quarter 1976. The application to Rudolf Bultmann's
theology, which appears on pp. 114-17, is also Professor
Hobbs's.

[18]This schematic diagram is from a document by Professor Hobbs and was first presented to two GTU doctoral seminars (PH 618 and RA 600a) during Fall Quarter 1976.

[19]Rudolf Bultmann, Existence and Faith, ed. and trans. Schubert M. Ogden (Cleveland and New York: Meridian Books, 1960), p. 87.

[20]Rudolf Bultmann, Theology of the New Testament, 2 vols., trans. Kendrick Grobel (New York: Charles Scribner's Sons, 1951 and 1955), 2:237.   Hereafter called TNT.

[21]Rudolf Bultmann, Faith and Understanding, ed. Robert W. Funk (New York: Harper and Row, 1966), p. 279.

[22]TNT, 2:238.

[23]Rudolf Bultmann, et al., Kerygma and Myth, ed. Hans Werner Bartsch, trans. Reginald H. Fuller (New York and Evanston: Harper & Row, 1961), p. 10, n. 2:   " . . . the use of imagery to express the other worldly in terms of this world and the divine in terms of human life, the other side in terms of this side. "

[24]This schematic diagram is by Professor Edward C. Hobbs, and was first circulated in various courses and programs during Winter Quarter 1977.

[25]These are the major sections of Bultmann's TNT.   The first major section, "The Message of Jesus," is not New Testament theology because it is not based on the Christian kerygma; it is the "presupposition" for New Testament theology (1:3).

[26]TNT, 2:180.

[27]Ibid., 2:175.

[28]Ibid., 2:141-42.

[29]For the history of Old Testament theology I am following Gerhard Hasel, Old Testament Theology: Basic Issues in the Current Debate, rev. ed. (Grand Rapids, Mich.:   Wm. B. Eerdmans, 1975), hereafter referred to by the name of the author, Hasel; supplemented by Georg Fohrer, History of Israelite Religion, trans. David E. Green (Nashville and New York: Abingdon Press, 1972), esp. pp. 17-25. Hasel gives

fuller bibliographic information for the older works mentioned in this section. He also says (p. 16) that the phrase "Biblical theology" first appeared in the no-longer-extant 1629 work by Wolfgang Jacob Christmann, Teutsche Biblische Theologie.

[30]Hasel, p. 20.

[31]J. P. Gabler, "Oratio de iusto discrimine theologicae biblicae et dogmaticae regundisque recte utriusque finibus," quoted in Hasel, p. 21.

[32]Hasel, p. 22.

[33]These examples are from Hasel, pp. 24-25.

[34]Examples of the "conservative reaction" scholars are G. F. Oehler and J. Ch. Konrad von Hofmann; Hasel, pp. 26-29.

[35]Hasel, pp. 29-30.

[36]For example, I. G. Matthews, The Religious Pilgrimage of Israel (New York: Harper, 1947).

[37]Georg Fohrer, History of Israelite Religion, pp. 21-22.

[38]Walter Eichrodt, Theology of the Old Testament, 2 vols., trans. J. A. Baker (Philadelphia: Westminster Press, 1961-67). The original German edition was published in 1933-39. Hereafter called Eichrodt.

[39]Eichrodt, 1:31, quoted in Hasel, p. 43.

[40]Eichrodt, 1:17, quoted in Hasel, p. 77.

[41]Eichrodt, 1:14 (emphasis his), quoted in Hasel, pp. 77-78.

[42]Gerhard von Rad, Old Testament Theology, 2 vols., trans. D. M. G. Stalker (Edinburgh: Oliver and Boyd; New York and Evanston: Harper & Row, 1962, 1965), 2:412. Hereafter called von Rad.

[43]These examples are from Hasel, pp. 79-80.

[44]Von Rad, 2:vii.

[45]Ibid., 1:115.

[46]Ibid., 2:415.

[47]Ibid., 1:105.

[48]Ibid., 1:106ff., 2:411.

[49]Ibid., 2:411-13.

[50]Ibid., 2:427.

[51]Hasel, pp. 85, 89.

[52]Von Rad, 2:viii.

[53]This summary is from Bultmann's Theology of the New Testament (TNT), 2:241-51.

[54]Biblische Theologie des Neuen Testaments (1911) and Neutestamentliche Theologie im Abriss dargestellt (1927), respectively.

[55]English translation: Jesus' Proclamation of the Kingdom of God, ed. and trans. Richard Hyde Hiers and David Larrimore Holland (Philadelphia: Fortress Press, 1971).

[56]TNT, 2:237. For a fuller discussion of Bultmann's understanding of New Testament theology see above, pp. 114-17.

[57]TNT, 2:238.

[58]Ibid.

[59]To repeat his table of contents: the "Earliest Church," the "Hellenistic Church Aside from Paul," "Paul," the "Gospel of John and the Johannine Epistles," the "Development toward the Ancient Church."

[60]Ulrich Wilckens, Weisheit und Torheit: eine exegetisch-religions-geschichtliche Untersuchung zu 1. Kor. 1 und 2 (Tübingen: J.C.B. Mohr, 1959); Dieter Georgi, Die Gegner des Paulus im 2. Korintherbrief: Studien zur religiösen Propaganda in der Spätantike, WMANT, XI (Neukirchen-Vluyn: Neukirchner Verlag, 1964); Walther Schmithals, Gnosticism in Corinth, trans. from 3d ed. (Nashville and New York: Abingdon Press, 1971).

[61]For an early call to the redactional approach see
Edward C. Hobbs, "A Different Approach to the Writing of
Commentaries on the Synoptic Gospels," in A Stubborn Faith:
Papers on Old Testament and Related Subjects Presented to
Honor William Andrew Irwin, ed. Edward C. Hobbs (Dallas:
Southern Methodist University Press, 1956).

[62]Edward C. Hobbs, The Gospel of Mark and the Exodus
(University of Chicago: Dissertation Series, 1952); "Death
and Resurrection ... That Rock Was Christ!" in motive,
April 1956, pp. 14-28; "Norman Perrin on Methodology in
the Interpretation of Mark: A Critique of 'The Christology of
Mark' and 'Toward an Interpretation of the Gospel of Mark,'"
in Christology and a Modern Pilgrimage: A Discussion with
Norman Perrin, ed. Hans Dieter Betz (Society of Biblical
Literature, 1971); Willi Marxsen, Mark the Evangelist, trans.
R. Harrisville (New York and Nashville: Abingdon Press,
1969); Philipp Vielhauer, "Erwägungen zur Christologie des
Markusevangeliums," Zeit und Geschichte, ed. Erich Dink-
ler (Tübingen: J.C.B. Mohr, 1964); T.J. Weeden, Mark--
Traditions in Conflict (Philadelphia: Fortress Press, 1971).

[63]Albert Schweitzer, The Quest of the Historical Jesus,
trans. W. Montgomery, with an introduction by James M.
Robinson (New York: Macmillan, 1968), p. 349.

[64]G. Bornkamm, G. Barth, and H. J. Held, Tradition
and Interpretation in Matthew (Philadelphia: Westminster
Press, 1963); Hans Conzelmann, The Theology of St. Luke
(New York: Harper & Row, 1960), German title: Die Mitte
der Zeit.

[65]Rudolf Bultmann, The Gospel of John, trans. G.R.
Beasley-Murray, R.W.N. Hoare, J.K. Richer (Philadelphia:
Westminster Press, 1971). The younger scholars include
two graduates of C.D.S.P.: Robert Fortna, The Gospel of
Signs: A Reconstruction of the Narrative Source Underlying
the Fourth Gospel (London: Cambridge University Press,
1970), and John L. Bogart, Orthodox and Heretical Perfectionism in the Johannine Community as Evident in the First
Epistle of John, SBL Dissertation Series Number 33 (Missoula, Mont.: Scholars Press, 1977).

[66]"Die Problematik einer Theologie des Neuen Testaments," ZThK, Beiheft 2 (September 1961), pp. 3-18; trans.
Jack Sanders, in The Bultmann School of Biblical Interpretation: New Directions?, vol. 1 of Journal for Theology and

the Church, Robert W. Funk, gen. ed. (New York: Harper & Row, Harper Torchbooks, 1965), pp. 169-83.   (God-language will be discussed below, in Chap. VI.)

[67]Ernst Käsemann, "The Problem of a New Testament Theology," New Testament Studies 19 (April 1973):235-45.

[68]Ibid., p. 245.

[69]Hans Conzelmann, An Outline of the Theology of the New Testament, trans. John Bowden (New York and Evanston: Harper & Row, 1969), hereafter called Conzelmann; and Werner George Kümmel, The Theology of the New Testament According to Its Major Witnesses: Jesus--Paul--John, trans. John E. Steely (Nashville and New York: Abingdon Press, 1973); hereafter called Kümmel.

[70]Conzelmann, p. xiii.

[71]Ibid., p. xv.

[72]Ibid., pp. xv-xvi.

[73]Kümmel, p. 18.

[74]Ibid., pp. 16-17.

[75]Ibid., p. 18.

[76]Ibid., p. 332.

[77]Ibid., p. 332.

[78]See above, pp. 114-17.

[79]Walter Bauer, Orthodoxy and Heresy in Earliest Christianity, ed. Robert A. Kraft and Gerhard Krodel, trans. a team from the Philadelphia Seminar on Christian Origins (Philadelphia: Fortress Press, 1971), pp. xxiii-xxiv; Rechtgläubigkeit und Ketzerei im ältesten Christentum, Beiträge zur historische Theologie, vol. 10 (Tübingen: Mohr/Siebeck, 1934). The English translation is from the 1965 German (2d) edition, which has minor corrections and added appendixes by Georg Strecker; some minor corrections and augmentations have been added to the English version (hereafter called O and H).

[80]O and H, pp. 38-39, and p. 39, nn. 91 and 93.

[81]Ibid., p. 21.

[82]Ibid., pp. 122-24.

[83]Ibid., pp. 112-17.

[84]Ibid., p. 231.

[85]Appendix 2, by Georg Strecker in the second German edition, and revised and augmented by Robert A. Kraft for the English edition, contains a discussion of the significant responses to the book, both for and against, up to that point.

[86]As an example of apparently antithetical surface structures in a totally different field, physicists sometimes picture light as a particle and sometimes as a wave.

[87]Ernst Troeltsch, Christian Thought: Its History and Application, ed. and with an introduction by Baron F. von Hügel (New York: Meridian Books, Living Age Books, 1957), p. 57. Hereafter called Christian Thought.

[88]Immanuel Kant, Gesammelte Schriften, herausgegeben von der königlich preussischen Akademie der Wissenschaften, Band 10: Briefwechsel (Berlin: 1900), pp. 152-53. Quoted in Ernst Troeltsch, The Absoluteness of Christianity and the History of Religions, trans. David Reid (Richmond, Va.: John Knox Press, 1971), p. 39. Hereafter called Absoluteness of Christianity.

[89]Absoluteness of Christianity, pp. 69-70.

[90]Ernst Troeltsch, "The Dogmatics of the Religionsgeschichtliche Schule," The American Journal of Theology 17 (January 1913): 17. Hereafter called "Dogmatics."

[91]Christian Thought, pp. 43-44.

[92]Geisteswissenschaften--for which there is no natural modern English translation--was Dilthey's German translation for an English original, John Stuart Mill's "moral sciences." Troeltsch discusses the two approaches at more length in Der Historismus und seine Probleme (Tübingen: J. C. B. Mohr [Paul Siebeck], 1922).

[93]Absoluteness of Christianity, pp. 87-88.

[94]Ibid., p. 87; also pp. 33-34.

[95]Ibid., pp. 30-31.

[96]Ibid., p. 71.

[97]Ibid., p. 107.

[98]Ibid., p. 118.

[99]Christian Thought, pp. 44-45.

[100]"Dogmatics," p. 19.

[101]Ibid., pp. 18-19.

[102]Much of this history of the ecumenical movement is from Williston Walker et al., A History of the Christian Church, 3d ed. (New York: Charles Scribner's Sons, 1970), pp. 338-57.

[103]Quoted in A Documentary History of the Faith and Order Movement 1927-1963, Lukas Vischer, ed. (St. Louis: Bethany Press, 1963), pp. 8-9 and p. 199, n. 1.

[104]The constitution of the World Council of Churches, Clause I, "Basis," 1948.   Quoted in Documents of the Christian Church, selected and edited by Henry Bettenson (London, Oxford, New York: Oxford University Press, 1963), p. 333. In 1961 at the Third Assembly of the World Council of Churches in New Delhi the wording was changed to this: "The World Council of Churches is a fellowship of Churches which confess the Lord Jesus Christ as God and Saviour according to the Scriptures and therefore seek to fulfil together their common calling to the glory of one God, Father, Son and Holy Spirit." Quoted in Bettenson, p. 334.

[105]Final Report: Third World Council on Faith and Order (Lund, 1952), § I. 2, quoted in A Documentary History of the Faith and Order Movement, p. 85.

[106]For a contemporary discussion of the theological impasse see Edward C. Hobbs, "The Ecumenical Movement: Its Theological Spirit," The Perkins School of Theology Journal 7 (Spring 1954): 6-8.

107Quoted in A History of the Christian Church, p. 546.

108Decree on Ecumenism, § I, 3.   Quoted from The Documents of Vatican II, ed. Walter M. Abbott, S. J. (New York: Guild Press, America Press, Association Press, 1966), pp. 345-46.   Hereafter called Vatican II.

109Ibid., § I, 4.   Vatican II, p. 347.

110Avery Dulles, S. J., "Introduction" [to Lumen Gentium], Vatican II, p. 11.

111Albert C. Outler, "Response" [to Lumen Gentium], Vatican II, p. 103.

112Ibid., p. 103.

113Gaudium et Spes, § 2; Vatican II, p. 200.

114Gaudium et Spes, § 62; Vatican II, p. 268.   Note 200, p. 268, by Donald R. Campion, S. J., adds, "This statement reveals the Council's own conviction that the notion of a theological 'aggiornamento' means more than a rephrasing of conventional theological teaching in contemporary terminology."

115Gaudium et Spes, § 74; Vatican II, p. 284.

116Gaudium et Spes, § 92; Vatican II, pp. 306-07.

117"Dogmatics," p. 21.

Chapter VI

GOD-LANGUAGE

The Issue

A major issue, perhaps the major issue, for contemporary theology is the so-called "problem of God." It is a problem that has been developing over many centuries--perhaps since the time of Constantine--but has come to focus only recently and has been explicitly recognized and agonized over only in the past few decades. It is the problem that meaningful use of the term "god/God"[1] is at least obsolescent in Western culture, if not already obsolete. There are pockets of God language in Western culture, of course, which may be excluded from that statement, for example the use of God-language in the discipline of theology and its (largely liturgical) use in churches and synagogues. But these are exceptions, and do not hold great importance for our culture at large. In earlier ages, the term was used meaningfully in ordinary discourse, and people could argue--meaningfully, they thought-- about God's actions, purposes, or qualities, or about the relative merits of one god as compared to another. They could even discuss whether or not God exists. But today it is not the existence of God that is problematic; it is not certain that the discussion can even rise to that level. What is problematic is any meaningful use at all of the term "God."

The attention of the Christian community was called to this problem in a way that could not be avoided in the early 1960s by the movement known as "radical theology" or "death-of-God theology." The slogan, "God is dead," taken from the proclamation of Nietzsche's "madman," was gloried in by some radical theologians and treated with suspicion by others, but they all helped to bring to light the issue of meaningful God-talk, or the failure of the term to function meaningfully today. One of the first in the movement was Gabriel Vahanian's The Death of God, [2] which dealt with what has happened to our culture in embodying the problem. A popular work that had a great impact on Christian lay people was Honest to God, by John A. T. Robinson, Bishop of Woolwich. [3] Another 1963 publication was The Secular Meaning of the Gospel, by Paul M. Van Buren. [4] In late 1963 William Hamilton wrote a survey of the radical theology movement up to that time, and it was published in 1965 as "The Death of God Theologies Today." [5] A Jewish version of death-of-God theology was done by Richard L. Rubenstein in After Auschwitz. [6] These works are only a small selection from the extensive discussion on the subject, which ran to many volumes and hundreds of articles. Samples of the response to the radical theologians can be found in, for example, Thomas W. Ogletree's The Death of God Controversy [7] and in Radical Theology: Phase Two, edited by C. W. Christian and Glenn R. Wittig. [8]

The death-of-God theologians were perhaps the most noticeable group dealing with the death of God, or at least with the death of God-language, but since their time others have continued working on the issue. A particularly interesting example is God the Problem, by Gordon Kaufman. [9] Others have attempted reconstructive responses--some directly to the death-of-God theologians, as in Langdon Gilkey's Naming the Whirlwind, [10] who provided an extensive analysis of the problem, as well as a suggested solution. Others who have worked somewhat independently of the death-of-God movement, who have tried to deal with the issue of the meaningfulness of the term without dealing directly with radical theology, are Schubert M. Ogden [11] and, in a lesser vein, John Macquarrie. [12] (Macquarrie dismisses the "death-of-God" theologians by ignoring most of them. Thomas Altizer and William Hamilton are not even mentioned, and Van Buren's theology is dismissed in the book's second paragraph as being "reduced" and therefore "no theology at all." [13]) All of these are merely a sampling of the current concern for the difficulty of showing the possibility of the meaningful use of the term "God" today.

We have learned from Wittgenstein that the meaning of a term is determined by its use. But if that standard is applied to the term "God" in our culture today, the chief meaning of "God" is as a feeling toner, used when the speaker wants to show his emotional involvement in his utterance. "God, it's hot today" expresses more feeling than the simple "It's hot today." "Jesus" and "Christ" are largely used as feeling toners also. (It is interesting that the God-language used as feeling toners usually shows more emotion than many other feeling toners--some of which are ground-down versions of old God-language--and certainly more than nothing, but they are not the strongest in common use today. The stronger ones are the "four-letter" words of sex and excretion, which have as a consequence suffered the same eclipse of meaningful use that God-language has.) Thus investigation of the meaning of "God" in terms of its use in the modern world seems to be blocked.

This was not the case in the ancient world, however, where the meaning of "god" (and the names of the individual gods) was greatly different from its "meaning" in today's world. When the ancient world spoke of "god" (or of a particular god), they meant something like what H. Richard Niebuhr called "the object of human faith in life's worthwhileness."[14] In Niebuhr's view all human beings live by faith, although they may not know it, or they do not live at all; human beings who do not choose to commit suicide are living their faith that life is worth living, or, as Niebuhr puts it, their "reliance on certain centers of value as able to bestow significance and worth on our existence."[15] It is from these centers that people derive their worth and for the sake of which they live.[16] There are many different value-centers-- Niebuhr also calls them "objects of loyalty," "causes," "objects of devotion," and "centers of worth"[17] --and human beings give allegiance to, or "faith in," many different such centers, even more than one at a time. No one value-center is common to all humanity; what is common is the structure of faith, the "attitude and action of confidence in, and fidelity to, certain realities as the sources of value and the objects of loyalty."[18] Human beings are not distinguished from one another by whether or not they "have faith," but by what they have faith in, by what value-center (or centers) they commit themselves to. Niebuhr points out that these value-centers--or more generally, these centers of faith in the worthwhileness of life--are called "gods." At least, they were called gods in the ancient world, when the term was still meaningful.

Niebuhr's interpretation of the original meaning of "God" as shown by its use has been expanded and clarified by Edward C. Hobbs.[19] Faith is "the commitment of one's future to X, a commitment made by response to whatever encounter requires decision and action."[20] The "X" in that definition stands for what the ancient world called a god, a center of ultimate meaning, or worth, or value, or purpose, or loyalty, or an ultimate good, or moral imperative, or even life-style--that is, the ultimate deciding factor in those fairly common situations that call for decision from human beings. "That for the sake of which one did what one did, ultimately, was one's god."[21] Or, as Luther put it, "Whatever then thy heart clings to ... and relies upon, that is properly thy God."[22] What one ultimately relies on as the focus of the worthwhileness of life--one's ultimate center of value, source of meaning, or goal of action--is one's "god," in the language of the ancient world.

If something like "the center of faith in the worthwhileness of life" is the original meaning of the term "God," then it is clear that what is at issue in the so-called "problem of God" is not the decline (if any) of religious language, or the need to find the right conceptualization of God. In the ancient world when the word "god" was used it was part of ordinary discourse, not relegated to a subset of language called "religious discourse"; it named the ultimate deciding factor called for in situations in any and all aspects of human life, not in some area of life, whether large or small, that can be categorized as "religious." Furthermore, it is the case that while the function of the term "God" remained constant, the conceptualizations of the gods held by the ancients--what they thought about their gods--varied considerably. Within the Old Testament alone, for example, the conceptualizations range from the God who enjoys walking in a cool garden in Genesis 3 to the "high and lofty One who inhabits eternity" of Isaiah 57. Adequate conceptualizations for today, therefore, though perhaps important, are not the primary problem. The issue is the disappearance of our ability to speak of that which God-language once brought to speech.

Chomsky's theory of language offers at least one way to gain insight into the problem, even though (as with pluralism in the preceding chapter) the solution is not yet worked out. When a language changes in the course of its development it does not usually lose any of its power to say what it once said. When one sort of transformation is eliminated (say, the morphological subjunctive in English) a different transformation (say, model auxiliaries) may be used, or invented, to form a new and different surface structure from the same deep structure. If God-language can be located in deep structure, then our loss of the particular transformations that in the past produced the word "God" and its synonyms in the surface structure may not mean the end of our ability to speak of what was once called "God"; other transformations of the same deep structure are possible, and may even be in use in the Western world today, although with their connection to God-language, of course, unrecognized. The question, then, is what sort of deep structure might lie behind surface-structure use of the term "God."[23]

The Proposal: Modality

It is the proposal of this chapter that the modality of sentences reveals the "gods" of their speakers. That is, while no single sentence adequately attests a particular god, the modality of a particular speaker's sentences overall will reveal a pattern or hierarchy or framework or structure of value or good that implies or even describes that speaker's "God" or "gods." In other words, much of our speaking attests to our choice of "gods," and thus the "God"-function in language is not lost, even when the noun "God" drops from the lexicon of our use.

In order to clarify this proposal, we must consider Chomsky's category "AUX." In Syntactic Structures Chomsky postulated the syntactic category "AUX," to provide a phrase-structure analysis of the English auxiliary verb. The relevant phrase-structure rules he suggested were these:

Verb → Aux + V

Aux → C (M) (have + en) (be + ing)[24]

C represented past tense and number; it was used in the obligatory "number transformation." M represented "modal"; its phrase-structure rule was M → will, can, may, shall, must. The parentheses represented optional elements, although the given order was required.

This picture was significantly modified in Aspects. The modifications of the understanding of the lexicon affected the lexical insertion of the modals, as was to be expected. But the principal difference, which Chomsky does not discuss, is that the phrase-structure rule that introduces "AUX" is now:

S → NP⏜Aux⏜VP[25]

But much later he creates the category "Predicate Phrase" to include both AUX and VP:

S → NP⏜Predicate Phrase

Predicate Phrase → Aux⏜VP (Place) (Time)[26]

The full rewrite rule for AUX appears to be:

Aux → Tense   (M) (Aspect)[27]

Various modifications and elaborations of this have been proposed,[28] and it is interesting that most of them cannot quite break the connection between "AUX" and V--despite Chomsky's moving AUX out of subordination to the VP.[29] No doubt old habits of English "auxiliary verbs" die hard. In terms of modals it means that only such modals as are expressed by English auxiliaries can be dealt with. Other "moods" must have different phrase-structure analyses. For example, it has been proposed that "imperative sentences in English form a special sentence-type, which has a basic phrase structure which is fundamentally different from regular declarative sentences."[30] It is different because it does not contain the category "AUX." Neither, incidentally, do infinitives or gerundives, and therefore, in this system, they cannot contain tense or modal either.[31]

The position that I am assuming with respect to "AUX" is Chomsky's own: that is, the independence of the "AUX" node from NP and VP. Thus the basic phrase structure rule is this:

S → NP + AUX + VP

In phrase-marker form:

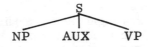

Further, I am assuming that the basic phrase-struc-

ture rule for AUX is this: AUX → Modal + Aspect + Time.
(I am using "Time" rather than "Tense" because "Tense" is
essentially a morphological category, often mingling aspect
and time.)   While it has little bearing on the proposal of this
chapter, I suspect that "Time" is the optional element, with
the other two obligatory, rather than the other way around as
in the Aspects proposal.   Thus, in phrase-marker form:

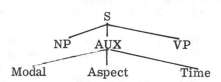

What is the "Modal" node?   It refers, of course, to
the "uncertain" sentence moods (suggested by such English
words as "may," "might," "can," "will," "must," etc.) but
also much more broadly to the "semantical mood" (as distinct from the "grammatical mood"[32]) of a sentence.

No theory of the "Modal" node (or of semantical mood)
commands anything like general assent.   For our purpose
we will explore one such theory, in order to exemplify one
way in which Chomsky's overall theory might illuminate our
problem.   That theory is the theory of "Mood Implicatures"
by Asa Kasher, who proposes to investigate moods in terms
of "generative pragmatics," that is, considering the relations
of speaker, sentence, and context (including the hearer, if
any.)[33]   This is a study of a part of linguistic competence
not performance; Kasher intends to describe ideal speakers,
who "never fail to perform happily speech acts they intend
to carry out. ...   In their discourse, preconditions never
fail to obtain and presuppositions are always true."[34]   They
always mean exactly what they say and believe what they assert; they never mislead or misunderstand.[35]   Making this
legitimate idealization, Kasher proposes to examine moods in
sentences.   He does not limit himself to sentences with clearly marked surface features, such as modal auxiliaries or
performative expressions; such sentences show their mood
more clearly than others.   But every sentence has a "semantical mood," as distinguished from a "grammatical mood,"
which may or may not be present.[36]   In effect Kasher is
saying that every sentence has a modal marker on the deep-
structure level, but that after transformation to the surface
structure level there may or may not be an overt modal feature remaining--and if there is, it may take various forms.

The division of every sentence into two logical elements, "(sentence) mood" and "(sentence) radical" (or "descriptive content," or "proposition") is not in itself anything
new; philosophers have been doing it at least since Frege,[37]
and linguists have used at least aspects of it ("Q" or "NEG"
as deep-structure markers, for example) long before Kasher
adopted it. But Kasher points out that no theory of moods
has yet been proposed that both characterizes each individual
mood and provides a general framework into which all the
different moods fit.   Kasher proposes to do both.

He first lays out some technical terminology, always
assuming an ideal speaker--one who only speaks when the
sentences are appropriate to the context.   One such technical
term is precondition.   One sentence (S') is said to be a precondition of another (S) is S' is believed by the speaker to
be true in the context of utterance of S, or true in the circumstances that are discussed in the context of utterance
(technically, in the exponent of the context).   Kasher distinguishes carefully between the context itself and the exponent
of the context, which is the possible state of affairs or circumstances (or any class of such states of affairs) fixed by
the context.   Thus he can distinguish between a context precondition and an exponent precondition when necessary.   For
example, an ideal speaker may utter the following sentence
(of course in an appropriate context):

S: Elsberg's present psychiatrist's former office is
     not in Washington.

The ideal speaker then must believe that the following sentence is true:

S':   There is presently exactly one psychiatrist who
      renders his professional services to Elsberg.[38]

S' is thus a precondition of S.   (In this case, as with all indicative sentences, S is also a precondition of itself.)

A precondition therefore involves a speaker's belief
that some sentence is true.   However, the hearer's beliefs
may also be involved, or rather, the speaker's beliefs about
the hearer's beliefs.   For an ideal speaker to speak appropriately in a particular context it cannot be required that the
hearer must believe that a particular sentence is true; if it
were, the speaker would have to have knowledge of the hearer's belief in order to speak appropriately.   But for the

speaker's own assertions, for example, it is enough that the
(ideal) speaker believe them to be true; an ideal speaker is
not required to be an omniscient being, or even an ideal
logician.   It may be the case, however, that for some utterances to be appropriate, the speaker may have to believe that
the hearer shares the speaker's preconditions (that is, beliefs).   For example, an ideal speaker could not use S above
if the speaker thought that the hearer believed S' to be false
--that is, that Elsberg does not presently use any psychiatrist, or that he presently uses more than one.   On the other
hand, the ideal speaker would also not use S if the speaker
believes that the hearer already believes it to be true.[39]   To
sum up, both S and S' are preconditions of S; but an ideal
speaker has to believe that the hearer believes S' to be true
but does not yet believe S to be true, in order to utter S
appropriately.   Although it is not illustrated by these particular examples, there is a third possibility: the speaker may
not have to have any belief about the hearer's belief in order to utter a sentence appropriately.

This discussion leads up to Kasher's definition of implicature.   S' is a strong context[40] implicature of S if S' is
a context precondition of S (i. e., the speaker believes S' to
be true in the context of S), and the speaker believes that
the hearer believes S' to be true in the context of S.   S' is
a weak context implicature of S if S' is a context precondition of S, and the speaker is not required to believe anything
about the hearer's beliefs.   Kasher expresses these definitions
in symbolic form, where α is the speaker, β is the hearer,
C is the appropriate context of utterance, and the expression
B (α, C, C, S') means that person α believes in C that S'
is true in C.   Then S' is a strong context implicature of S
if B (α, C, C, S') & B (α, C, C, B (β, C, C, S')).   S' is
a weak context implicature of S if B (α, C, C, S') & $\sim$ B
(α, C, C, B, (β, C, C, S')) & $\sim$ B (α, C, C, $\sim$ B (β, C, C, S')).[41]

With these tools in hand Kasher now turns to moods.
Since a sentence can be characterized as sentence radical
and sentence mood, every utterance consists of the speaker's
choice of radical and choice of what use to put the radical to.
When putting a radical to a particular use--linguistically
speaking, when choosing a (semantical) mood--a speaker is
indicating that a radical participates in some particular standard relations.   It is Kasher's contention that "the standard
relations are preference relations exclusively."[42]   In each
choice of mood the speaker conveys a preference for one state
of affairs over some other that differs from the preferred

one only in some relevant respect. Furthermore, Kasher claims that an appropriate preference relation for any given sentence is both a context precondition and a weak context implicature of that sentence. (That is, the speaker will believe that the preference relation is true in the context, but will not necessarily have any opinion about whether the hearer believes it to be true or not. To put it another way, the speaker will believe him- or herself to prefer one particular state of affairs over another, but what the speaker thinks the hearer believes about the speaker's preference is irrelevant.)

To take an example, suppose an ideal speaker utters the command, "Give me the file marked confidential" to a hearer. The preference relation states that, given two states of affairs that differ only in that in the first the hearer hands the speaker the file and in the second does not, the speaker prefers the first. Or, to be exact, the speaker believes that he or she prefers the first; since the speaker is only an ideal speaker, not an ideal logician, and may be mistaken.

Thus the preference relation is a context precondition; the speaker believes it to be true. The preference relation is also a weak context implicature, because the speaker's opinions about the hearer's belief about what the speaker prefers are irrelevant to the appropriate utterance of the command. Usually, when an ideal speaker says, "Give me the file marked confidential" to an ideal hearer, the speaker does not assume that the hearer knows what the speaker wants. But the latter might use the command in a situation in which he or she does assume that the hearer already knows what the speaker wants--for example, to a hearer who is refusing to obey the speaker.[43] Kasher concludes that this structure of preference relation is applicable to all semantically imperative sentences, regardless of whether they contain an explicit performative ("I hereby order you to give me the file marked confidential"), a grammatical imperative ("Give me the file marked confidential"), or some other transformation.

To state the preference relation, Kasher introduces the notation $\text{PREF}_{\alpha, C}(a, b)$, which means that in context C, α prefers state of affairs a to state of affairs b. α and β are speaker and hearer, as before; when it is necessary to distinguish them, C_1 is the context of utterance and C_2 is a context immediately following it; $B_{\alpha, C}$ stands for what α believes about C, at C, and $K_{\alpha, C}$ stands for what α knows about C, at C.   p is the radical of the original sentence, roughly, in this example, "that α give β the file marked confidential." Then, in the case we have been discussing: "Give me the file marked confidential" the preference relation can be written as

$$S': \quad PREF_{\alpha, C_1} \, (p, \, \sim p).$$

Using this notation, Kasher suggests some preference relations involved in some other semantical moods.[44]

S: Did you give me the file marked confidential?

$$S': \quad PREF_{\alpha, C_1} \, (v_1, \, v_2)$$

$$v_1 \text{ is } [B_{\alpha, C_1}(K_{\beta, C_1}p \, v \, K_{\beta, C_1}\sim p), \, K_{\alpha, C_2} \, p \, v \, K\alpha, \, C_2 \sim p]$$

$$v_2 \text{ is } [B_{\alpha, C_1}(K_{\beta, C_1}p \, v \, K_{\beta, C_1}\sim p), \sim K\alpha, C_2 \, p \, v \, K_{\alpha, C_2} \sim p]$$

Roughly translated, this means that the speaker, believing that the hearer knows the answer to the question, prefers the situation in which the answer is also known to the speaker (a short while later) to the situation in which it is not.[45]

S: She gave me the file marked confidential.

$$S': \quad PREF_{\alpha, C} \, (v_1, \, v_2)$$

$$v_1 \text{ is } [B_{\alpha, C_1} \, p, \, K_{\beta}, \, C_2 \, B_{\alpha, C_1} p]$$

$$v_2 \text{ is } [B_{\alpha, C_1} \, p, \, \sim K_{\beta}, C_2 \, B_{\alpha, C_1} p]$$

Here the speaker believes the assertion, and prefers the situation in which the hearer knows (a little later) that the speaker believes it over the situation in which the hearer does not know that the speaker believes it.

S: If you don't give me the file marked confidential,
      I shall dismiss you.

$$S': \quad PREF_{\alpha, C}(r, \sim r) \quad \& \quad PREF_{\alpha, C}([\sim r, \, q], \, [\sim r, \sim q])$$

(In this case, the radical is analyzed into components--p: if r,q). This is a double preference: the speaker prefers getting the file to not getting it, and also prefers not getting the file and dismissing the hearer to not getting the file and not dismissing the hearer.

S: I advise you to give me the file marked confidential.

S': $\text{PREF}_{\alpha, C_1}(v_1, v_2)$

v_1 is $\text{PREF}_{\beta, C_2}(p, {\sim}p)$

v_2 is $\text{PREF}_{\alpha, C_2}({\sim}p, p)$

Here the speaker prefers the situation in which the hearer prefers to give the speaker the file over not giving the speaker the file, to the situation in which the hearer's preferences are reversed.   All of these preference relations are context preconditions and weak context implicatures of their sentences.

Kasher says that at least some of these preference relation statements have to be amended, although not fundamentally.   For example, in many cases the internal structure of the radicals may have to be considered in the statement of a preference relation.   Otherwise the statement of the preference relation implicated by a promise will appear identical to that of the command discussed above.   (Of course, the preference relation for the command would have to be similarly amended.)   Even after this is worked out there may still be some apparently different semantical moods that seem to have similarly structured preference relations, for example, demands, requests, and commands.   Kasher suggests two more possibilities for distinguishing them.   One is to take into account the intensity of the mood.   (He proposes to call such cases different speech acts and semantical moods that share their preference relation structure but not their intensities; he acknowledges, however, that one could say that they are the same mood with different intensity.)   The second possibility is to add, in some cases, a strong context implicature to the situations described in the preference relation.   In the case of a command (as distinguished from, say, a request) α believes that he/she is in a position of authority over β, and believes that β also believes that α is in a position of authority over β.   Then the command

S: Give me the file marked confidential

has the preference relation

S': $\text{PREF}_{\alpha, C_1}(v_1, v_2)$

where v_1 is $[p, q]$ and v_2 is $[{\sim}p, q]$.   The notation is the same

as above, with the addition of the proposition q: "that α is
in a position to command β at C."

Various consequences can be deduced from this and
the other basic preference relations, which are all weak context implicatures of their original sentences. But for each
semantical mood there is one basic preference relation (of
some degree of intensity); each basic preference relation is
called a <u>pragmeme</u>. It is interesting that each pragmeme is
a <u>weak</u> context implicature, not a strong one; it is a statement about the speaker's beliefs, and thus no hearer is necessary for the explication of modality (although of course a
hearer may appear in the propositional content of a particular sentence).

While Kasher has built his theory around what he has
labeled the speaker's "preference," he does not mean to
limit himself to the mild liking that the English word may
connote. While in some cases a mere liking may be involved,
in most real cases Kasher says specifically that a preference relation is usually backed by other preference relations
that "constitute [the speaker's] general purposes and plans."[46]
Thus Kasher takes preference relations to be statements of
the speaker's "goals," "purposes," and "plans"; other terms
that seem legitimate (although Kasher does not use them)
might be speaker's values, will (or volition), or ideals, or
concerns, or commitments--and many others. This, plus
the fact that Kasher allows for different intensities of preference relations, shows that preference relations can operate at all levels of importance to the speaker.

We are now in a position to see how Chomsky's theory,
when developed in terms of the AUX node and the Modal sub-
node, fulfills our need to locate the "God-problem" in deep
structure. Kasher has shown that every sentence, whatever
its "grammatical mood," has a "semantical mood." The
"semantical mood" chosen by the speaker exhibits the preference relations that the sentence radical participates in.
Thus <u>every</u> sentence (even semantically "indicative" sentences,
although the implications of this will not be explored here)
exhibits a preference relation. This means that each sentence contains in its deep structure a feature expressing the
preference relation of the sentence, which reveals what the
speaker regards as possessing value or worth--or, in Kasher's language, what is to be preferred in the context of
that utterance. <u>Particular</u> choices as to goods or values are
thus implicated in every utterance. However, since Niebuhr

has shown that what we mean by "God" is the center of value
(or centers of value, i.e., "gods") in human life, and since
this center or these centers are the ultimate deciding factors
when humans are called upon to make choices or decisions,
it is clear that every "preference relation" (that is, every
acknowledgment of better/worse, good/bad, value/disvalue)
has a place in a structure or hierarchy of preference--or
values or goods.

(It is interesting, although coincidental, that Ian Ramsey independently used the same term "preference" in Models
for Divine Activity.[47]   This work was based on the Zenos
Lectures at McCormick Theological Seminary in Chicago,
which Ramsey delivered in March 1966; Ramsey died in October 1972, and the lectures were published posthumously in
1973.   In them Ramsey uses precisely the same term "preference" to refer to the choice "between alternative views of
the universe--ways of looking at the world."[48]   Hence Kasher's choice of the term "preference" is not wholly unrelated
to the language used by theologians to discuss the meaning
of "God.")

The particular preferences exhibited by a speaker in
every utterance are clearly interrelated.   In every case a
chain of preferences could theoretically be pursued: the
speaker prefers A to B, because A will lead to P rather than
Q, and the speaker prefers P to Q because P will lead to
X rather than Y, etc.   This chain of preferences points to
preference behind which, for that speaker, there is no further choice, a preference that is ultimately decisive, not referring to anything beyond itself.   This, of course, is the
point at which we reach "God" for the speaker/chooser/pre-
ferrer.   Thus implicit in every preference relation is a further, or perhaps prior, preference relation; and it is these
relationships that are in fact a structure of value or good.

To conclude, whether we like it or not, and whether
we know it or not, our preferences are implicated in our
every action of speaking.   Since preferences are another name
for the value/worth/good game, it is difficult to avoid the
conclusion that implicit in the use of human language itself
is the choice among the "gods."   The real "God-language-
game" is thus not when people use the word "God," but when-
ever people use sentences at all.   Although most sentences
involve ultimate preference (that is, "God") only remotely,
nevertheless, a speaker's overall linguistic performance is
not only dependent on, but revelatory of, that speaker's God or
pantheon.

This is analogous to, and perhaps even actually connected with, the interrelationship between an individual's "performance" and that person's "competence" in language. No particular sentence reveals or even necessitates the entire grammar of a language; but without the grammar to generate the strings that result in sentences there can be no individual sentences. And while it is true that there may be no "discovery procedures" by which we can infallibly infer the grammar of a language from the "corpus" of all its known sentences, we nevertheless use those actual sentences to test our theories about that grammar. Similarly, no "discovery procedure" for inferring a person's theology from that person's utterances is here suggested; but if ultimate preference or preferences are involved in lesser or more immediate preferences, then we may at least hypothesize that the sentences uttered by an individual or a community will provide suitable tests for a theory as to the individual's or the community's God(s). Further, we are justified in doing so despite the absence of a usable group of nouns meaning "God."

Thus Chomsky's revolution in linguistics, developed in terms of the modal structure of sentences, whether along Kasher's lines or others, helps to bring to light and make available for discussion that dimension of human existence formerly named by the names of the gods. Now it is up to the theologians to take advantage of this possibility.

Notes

[1] The capitalization requirements of English pose problems here. In what follows I will arbitrarily use "God" (unless the context clearly calls for "god"), but without necessarily meaning anything by the upper-case "G."

[2] Gabriel Vahanian, The Death of God (New York: G. Braziller, 1961).

[3] John A. T. Robinson, Honest to God (London: SCM Press; Philadelphia: Westminster Press, 1963).

[4] Paul M. Van Buren, The Secular Meaning of the Gospel, Based on an Analysis of Its Language (New York: Macmillan, 1963). This work was mentioned above, p. 104.

[5] William Hamilton, "The Death of God Theologies To-

day," in The Christian Scholar 48 (Spring 1965):   27-48; reprinted in Radical Theology and the Death of God, ed.   Thomas
J. J. Altizer and William Hamilton (Indianapolis, New York,
and Kansas City: Bobbs-Merrill, 1966), pp. 23-50.

[6]Richard Rubenstein, After Auschwitz: Radical Theology and Contemporary Judaism (Indianapolis, New York,
and Kansas City: Bobbs-Merrill, 1966).

[7]Thomas W. Ogletree, The Death of God Controversy
(Nashville and New York: Abingdon Press, 1966).

[8]C. W. Christian and Glenn R. Wittig, eds., Radical
Theology: Phase Two (Philadelphia and New York: J. B.
Lippincott, 1967).

[9]Gordon Kaufman, God the Problem (Cambridge, Mass.:
Harvard University Press, 1972).

[10]Langdon Gilkey, Naming the Whirlwind: The Renewal
of God-Language (Indianapolis and New York: Bobbs-Merrill,
1969).

[11]Schubert M. Ogden, The Reality of God and Other
Essays (New York: Harper & Row, 1966).

[12]John Macquarrie, God-Talk: An Examination of the
Language and Logic of Theology (New York and Evanston:
Harper & Row, 1967).

[13]Ibid., pp. 11-12.

[14]H. Richard Niebuhr, Radical Monotheism and Western
Culture, with Supplementary Essays (New York, Evanston,
and London: Harper & Row, 1960), p. 119.

[15]Radical Monotheism, p. 118.

[16]Ibid., p. 21.

[17]Ibid., pp. 16, 24, 118.

[18]Ibid., p. 16.

[19]In particular, see Edward C. Hobbs, "A Theology of
the Arts," in The Church, Entertainment Media and Moral
Values, ed.   Donald Kuhn (Television, Radio, and Film Com-

mission; The Division of Temperance and General Welfare of the General Board of Christian Social Concerns of the Methodist Church, 1962), pp. 6-10; "An Alternate Model from a Theological Perspective," in The Family in Search of a Future, ed. Herbert A. Otto (New York: Appleton-Century-Crofts, 1970), pp. 25-41; "Gospel Miracle Story and Modern Miracle Stories," in Gospel Studies in Honor of Sherman Elbridge Johnson, ed. Massey H. Shepherd and Edward C. Hobbs, Anglican Theological Review, Supplementary Series (March 1974), no. 3, pp. 117-26.

[20]"An Alternative Model from a Theological Perspective," p. 25.

[21]"Gospel Miracle Story and Modern Miracle Stories," p. 119.

[22]Quoted in Radical Monotheism, p. 119.

[23]The next section of the paper will deal with the use of "generic" God-language, one way in which Chomsky's theory of language may illuminate the problem. But there is at least one other way that seems highly promising: the use of his theory of nominalization to illuminate the structure of specific God-language, that is, language about a particular God, and to make a distinction between God-language, in the Judeo-Christian tradition and pagan God-language. It may be the case that, given the necessary structure for any God-language at all (to be discussed in the next section), specific God-language may be a nominalization, a rewrite (as an NP) of a sentence. In the case of the pagan gods the sentence embedded seems to have been an equative, with value-meaning-purpose equated with a quality--e. g., law and order, fertility, home and family, rationality, power, pleasure, love, sex, and beauty, etc. Thus, for example, a deep structure sentence such as "the focus of the worthwhileness of life is law and order" could be transformed into "Zeus" in the ancient Greek world. In pagan society what was worthy of trust and gave value to living could be expressed as a quality--different qualities for different gods.
    The God of Israel was not defined in terms of some particular quality--a good or value, for example--but in terms of all that happened. In other words, Israel did not choose out of history certain things that God was responsible for (such as law and order), leaving other things under the control of, say, the devil. Rather, everything that happened offered human beings the possibility of good; all life was

worthy of trust, even under such circumstances as the fall of Jerusalem and the Exile. Linguistically, the Biblical tradition (and, following that, the Christian liturgical tradition) talked about God in nonequative sentences, usually with active verbs. This God "brought you out of the land of Egypt," "raised Christ Jesus from the dead," has "caused all holy Scriptures to be written for your learning," has "safely brought us to the beginning of this day." Active, nonequative sentences like these are nominalized into "Yahweh," "the God and Father of Jesus Christ," or simply "God." The locus of ultimate concern in the pagan tradition is a quality; in the Biblical tradition, an event that has happened or is happening. This difference expresses itself in the embedded sentences (equative or nonequative) that, in the presence of the other appropriate conditions for God-language, could undergo the particular nominalizing transformation that introduced the name of a particular god.

²⁴Structures, p. 11.

²⁵Aspects, p. 68. This point is repeated on pp. 69, 72, 79, and 86. Also see his extended discussion in n. 9, p. 212.

²⁶Ibid., p. 102.

²⁷Ibid., p. 107.

²⁸Some recent examples are R. Jackendoff, Semantic Interpretation in Generative Grammar (Cambridge, Mass.: MIT Press, 1972); J. Edmonds, A Transformational Approach to English Syntax (New York: Academic Press, 1976); P. Culicover, Syntax (New York: Academic Press, 1976); A. Akmajian and T. Wasow, "The Constituent Structure of VP and AUX and the Position of the Verb BE," Linguistic Analysis 1 (1975): 205-45.

²⁹Another type of analysis entirely treats English auxiliaries as main verbs with suitably constrained sentential complements. This was originally proposed by J. Ross, "Auxiliaries as Main Verbs," Studies in Philosophical Linguistics, Series 1, ed. W. Todd (Evanston, Ill.: Great Expectations Press, 1967).

³⁰Adrian Akmajian, Susan M. Steele, Thomas Wasow, "The Category AUX in Universal Grammar," June 1977. Xeroxed copy. The authors say they are following S.

Schmerling, "The Syntax of English Imperatives, " University
of Texas papers, 1977.

[31]Ibid. , p. 45. Although tense is not the issue here,
this shows the straitjacket that traditional terminology has
imposed. Since infinitives and gerundives do have varying
forms (the infinitive example on this page is "For you to
have been reading the private diary [was rude], " traditionally
called perfect progressive), I presume that the "tense" they
are said not to contain could better be called "time. "

[32]The terms are those of E. Stenius (see below, n. 36).
Asa Kasher prefers the terms "pragmatical mood" and "syntactical mood" (discussed in the next portion of the chapter).

[33]Asa Kasher, "Mood Implicatures: A Logical Way of
Doing Generative Pragmatics, " Theoretical Linguistics 1
(1974): 6-38. Hereafter called Kasher.

[34]Ibid. , p. 7.

[35]Ibid. , pp. 21, 33.

[36]These terms were introduced by E. Stenius, Wittgenstein's "Tractatus" (Oxford, England: Basil Blackwell, 1964),
p. 168.

[37]Gottlob Frege, "The Thought: A Logical Inquiry, "
1918/19, in Philosophical Logic, ed. P. F. Strawson (London: Oxford University Press, 1967), pp. 17-38. Cited by
Kasher, p. 12.

[38]These examples are from Kasher, p. 21.

[39]This "maxim of precluded superfluity" is characteristic of ideal speakers. Kasher, p. 22.

[40]Kasher also defines exponent implicatures, which substitute exponent for context; however, they do not figure in
his description of moods, so I will disregard them here.

[41]Kasher, p. 23.

[42]Ibid. , p. 25.

[43]The hearer may deduce the speaker's preference from
the fact of the command, and may even, since only an ideal

hearer and not necessarily an ideal cooperator, use this information against the speaker. Kasher calls this the "communication price." Kasher, p. 33 and references there.

[44]Kasher, pp. 28-29. I have corrected a couple of misprints. I am also omitting one example that involves an exponent and is not needed for the exposition.

[45]For convenience I am providing these "translations," but they are not as precise as Kasher's formulas. More precision is possible but does not seem necessary in this context.

[46]Kasher, p. 27.

[47]Ian T. Ramsey, Models for Divine Activity (London: SCM Press, 1973).

[48]Ibid., p. 58.

CONCLUSION

In this book I have investigated a major new intellectual system, transformational-generative linguistics, primarily developed by Noam Chomsky. I have set Chomsky's work in the context of his predecessors in the field of linguistics, through his teacher Zellig S. Harris. I have described the revolution that Chomsky has brought about in the field of linguistics and noted a few of the effects it has had on other fields. And I have examined some reactions of thinkers in other fields and Chomsky's responses to those reactions.

Turning to theology, I have suggested that theology has always used models of one sort or another and that it has always had close links with language and with theories or at least understandings of language. Therefore, I suggested, it is plausible that Chomsky's work may provide a viable and even elegant model for doing theology in our own time. I have taken two theological problems, pluralism and God-language, and shown their importance for contemporary theology. After discussing other efforts to deal with the problems, I have then suggested how they may be illuminated in new ways by Chomsky's theory of language and mind, as supplemented by certain other thinkers, especially the comparative mythologist Georges Dumézil.

The utility and elegance of the transformational-generative model of Noam Chomsky is what I hope I have shown. Its power remains to be demonstrated by further theological work.

SELECTED BIBLIOGRAPHY

I. Linguistics and Language

Akmajian, Adrian; Steele, Susan M.; and Wasow, Thomas.
"The Category AUX in Universal Grammar." (Xeroxed.)

Akmajian, A., and Wasow, T. "The Constituent Structure
of VP and AUX and the Position of the Verb BE."
Linguistic Analysis 1 (1975): 205-45.

Arnauld, Antoine, and Lancelot, Claude. General and Rational Grammar: The Port-Royal Grammar. Edited
and translated by Jacques Rieux and Bernard E. Rollin.
With a preface by Arthur C. Dante. With a critical
essay by Norman Kretzmann. The Hague: Mouton,
1977. (Originally published in 1660.)

Austin, John L. How to Do Things with Words. 2d ed.
Cambridge, Mass.: Harvard University Press, 1975.

Bach, Emmon. "Comments on the Paper by Chomsky." In
Formal Syntax, pp. 135-55. Edited by Peter W. Culi-
cover, Thomas Wasow, and Adrian Akmajian. New
York: Academic Press, 1977.

Bloomfield, Leonard. Language. New York: Holt, Rinehart and Winston, 1933.

Bresnan, Joan. "On the Form and Functioning of Transformations." Linguistic Inquiry 7 (1976): 3-40.

_____. "Sentence Stress and Syntactic Transformations." Language 47 (1971): 257-81.

_____. "Transformations and Categories in Syntax." Proceedings of the Fifth International Congress on Logic, Methodology, and the Philosophy of Science. University of Western Ontario, London, Ontario, 1975. Edited by R. Butts and J. Hintikka. In press.

Chomsky, Noam. Aspects of the Theory of Syntax. Cambridge, Mass.: MIT Press, 1965.

_____. Cartesian Linguistics. New York and London: Harper & Row, 1966.

_____. Essays on Form and Interpretation. New York: Elsevier North-Holland, 1977.

_____. "The Formal Nature of Language." In Studies in General and Oriental Linguistics Presented to Shiro Hattori on the Occasion of his Sixtieth Birthday. Edited by Roman Jacobson and Shigeo Kawamoto. Tokyo: TEC Co., 1970. Reprinted in Studies on Semantics in Generative Grammar, by Noam Chomsky, pp. 62-119, and in Semantics, edited by D.D. Steinberg and L.A. Jakobovits, pp. 183-216.

_____. "Language and Freedom." Lecture, 1970. In For Reasons of State. New York: Vintage Books, 1973.

_____. Language and Mind. Enlarged edition. New York: Harcourt Brace Jovanovich, 1972.

_____. Language and Responsibility. Based on conversations with Mitsou Ronat. Translated by John Viertel. New York: Pantheon Books, 1977.

_____. The Logical Structure of Linguistic Theory. New York: Plenum Press, 1975.

_____. "On Wh-Movement." In Formal Syntax, pp. 71-132. Edited by Peter W. Culicover, Thomas Wasow, and Adrian Akmajian. New York: Academic Press, 1977.

_____. Problems of Knowledge and Freedom. New York: Vintage Books, 1971.

_____. Reflections on Language. New York: Random House, 1975.

_____. "Remarks on Nominalization." In Readings in English Transformational Grammar. Edited by Roderick A. Jacobs and Peter S. Rosenbaum. Waltham, Mass.: Ginn, 1970. Reprinted in Studies on Semantics in Generative Grammar, by Noam Chomsky, pp. 11-61.

_____. "A Review of B. F. Skinner's Verbal Behavior." Language 35 (1959): 26-58. Reprinted in The Structure of Language, edited by J. A. Fodor and J. J. Katz, pp. 547-78.

_____. "Rules and Representations." Immanuel Kant Lectures, 1979. Stanford University. 8-18 January 1979. Now published as Part I of:

_____. Rules and Representations. New York: Columbia University Press, 1980.

_____. Studies on Semantics in Generative Grammar. The Hague: Mouton, 1972.

_____. Syntactic Structures. The Hague: Mouton, 1957.

_____. "Three Models for the Description of Language." I. R. E. Transactions on Information Theory. Vol. IT-2, no. 3. Proceedings of the Symposium on Information Theory Held at M. I. T. September 1956.

_____. Topics in the Theory of Generative Grammar. The Hague and Paris: Mouton, 1966.

_____, and Halle, Morris. Sound Patterns in English. New York: Harper & Row, 1968.

_____, and Lasnik, Howard. "Filters and Control." Linguistic Inquiry 8 (Summer 1977): 425-504.

Culicover, P. Syntax. New York: Academic Press, 1976.

Emonds, J. A Transformational Approach to English Syntax. New York: Academic Press, 1976.

Fillmore, C. J. "The Position of Embedding Transformations in a Grammar." Word 19 (1963): 208-31.

Fodor, J. A., and Katz, J. J., eds. The Structure of Language: Readings in the Philosophy of Language. Englewood Cliffs, N. J.: Prentice-Hall, 1964.

Gleason, H. A. Linguistics and English Grammar. New York: Holt, Rinehart and Winston, 1965.

Grice, H. P. "Utterer's Meaning and Intentions." Philosophical Review 78 (1969): 147-77.

_____. "Utterer's Meaning, Sentence-Meaning, and Word-Meaning." Foundations of Language 4 (1968): 225-42. Reprinted in The Philosophy of Language, pp. 54-70. Edited by John R. Searle. London: Oxford University Press, 1971.

Grinder, John T., and Elgin, Suzette Haden. Guide to Transformational Grammar: History, Theory, Practice. New York: Holt, Rinehart and Winston, 1973.

Harris, Zellig S. "Co-Occurrence and Transformation in Linguistic Structure." Language 33 (1957): 283-340.

_____. "Discourse Analysis." Language 28 (1952): 1-30.

_____. "From Morpheme to Utterance." Language 22 (1946): 161-83.

_____. Methods of Structural Linguistics. Chicago: University of Chicago Press, 1951.

Hornstein, N. "S and the X̄ Convention." Montreal Working Papers in Linguistics 4: 35-71.

Jackendoff, R. Semantic Interpretation in Generative Grammar. Cambridge, Mass.: MIT Press, 1972.

_____. X̄ Syntax: A Study of Phrase Structure. Linguistic Inquiry Monographs 2. Cambridge, Mass.: MIT Press, forthcoming.

Kasher, Asa. "Mood Implicatures: A Logical Way of Doing Generative Pragmatics." Theoretical Linguistics 1 (1974): 6-38.

Katz, J. J.   "Logic and Language: An Examination of Recent
    Criticism of Intentionalism."   In Minnesota Studies in
    Philosophy of Science, vol. 6.   Edited by Gunderson,
    Keith, and Grover.   Minneapolis: University of Min-
    nesota Press, 1975.

_____.   Propositional Structure and Illocutionary Force:
    A Study of the Contribution of Sentence Meaning to
    Speech Acts.   Hassocks, England: Harvester, 1977.

_____.   Semantic Theory.   New York: Harper & Row,
    1972.

_____, and Fodor, J. A.   "The Structure of a Semantic
    Theory."   Language 39 (1963):   170-210.   Reprinted in
    The Structure of Language, pp. 469-518.   Edited by
    Katz and Fodor.

_____, and Postal, P. M.   An Integrated Theory of Lin-
    guistic Descriptions.   Cambridge, Mass.:   MIT Press,
    1964.

Klima, E. S.   "Negation in English."   In The Structure of
    Language, pp. 246-323.   Edited by J. A. Fodor and
    J. J. Katz.

Lakoff, George.   "On Generative Semantics."   In Semantics,
    pp. 232-96.   Edited by Danny D. Steinberg and Leon
    A. Jakobovits.

Lakoff, Robin.   "Review of Grammaire générale et raisonnée."
    Language 45 (1969):   343-64.

Lees, Robert.   The Grammar of English Nominalizations.
    The Hague: Mouton, 1960.

_____.   "Review of Noam Chomsky's Syntactic Structures."
    Language 33 (1957):   375-408.   Reprinted in On Noam
    Chomsky, pp.   34-79.   Edited by G. Harmon.

Lyons, John.   Introduction to Theoretical Linguistics.   Cam-
    bridge, England: Cambridge University Press, 1971.

_____.   Noam Chomsky.   New York: Viking Press, 1970.

McCawley, James D.   "Where do noun phrases come from?"
    In Semantics, pp. 217-31.   Edited by Danny D. Stein-
    berg and Leon A. Jakobovits.

McClay, Howard. "Overview." In Semantics, pp. 157-82.
    Edited by Danny D. Steinberg and Leon A. Jakobovits.

Robbins, R. H.   General Linguistics: An Introductory Survey.
    London: Longmans, Green, 1964.

Ross, J.   "Auxiliaries as Main Verbs."   Studies in Philo-
    sophical Linguistics, Series 1.   Edited by W. Todd.
    Evanston, Ill.:   Great Expectations Press, 1967.

Sapir, Edward.   Language: An Introduction to the Study of
    Speech.   New York: Harcourt, Brace, 1921.

Saussure, Ferdinand de.   Course in General Linguistics.
    Edited by Charles Bally and Albert Sechehaye in col-
    laboration with Albert Riedlinger.   Translated by Wade
    Baskin.   New York: Philosophical Library: McGraw-
    Hill, 1966.   (Original French edition published in 1915.)

Searle, John R.   "Chomsky's Revolution in Linguistics."
    The New York Review of Books, 1972.   Reprinted in
    On Noam Chomsky, pp. 2-33.   Edited by G. Harmon.

_____.   "The Rules of the Language Game"   Times Liter-
    ary Supplement.   London, 10 September 1976.

_____.   Speech Acts: An Essay in the Philosophy of
    Language.   Cambridge, England: Cambridge University
    Press, 1969.

Steinberg, Danny D., and Jakobovits, Leon A., eds.   Seman-
    tics: An Interdisciplinary Reader in Philosophy, Lin-
    guistics, and Psychology.   Cambridge, England: Cam-
    bridge University Press, 1971.

Whorf, Benjamin Lee.   Language, Thought, and Reality.
    Edited by John B. Carroll.   Cambridge, Mass.:   MIT
    Press, 1956.

Wittgenstein, Ludwig.   The Blue and Brown Books.   New
    York: Harper & Row, 1958.

_____.   Philosophical Investigations.   3d edition.   Trans-
    lated by G. E. M. Anscombe.   New York: Macmillan,
    1953.

II. Theology and Religion

Abbott, Walter M., S.J., ed. The Documents of Vatican II.
New York: Guild Press, America Press, Association
Press, 1966.

Altizer, Thomas J.J., and Hamilton, William, eds. Radical
Theology and the Death of God. Indianapolis, New
York, and Kansas City: Bobbs-Merrill, 1966.

Augustine. The Confessions of Saint Augustine. Translated
by F.J. Sheed. London and New York: Sheed and
Ward, 1944.

Bauer, Walter. Orthodoxy and Heresy in Earliest Christianity. Translated by a team from the Philadelphia
Seminar on Christian Origins. Edited by Robert A.
Kraft and Gerhard Krodel. Philadelphia: Fortress
Press, 1971. Original German edition: Rechtgläubigkeit
und Ketzerei im ältesten Christentum. In Beiträge zur
historische Theologie, vol. 10. Tübingen: Mohr/Sie-
beck, 1934.

Bettensen, Henry, ed. Documents of the Christian Church.
2d ed. London, Oxford, New York: Oxford University
Press, 1963.

Bogart, John L. Orthodox and Heretical Perfectionism in the
Johannine Community as Evident in the First Epistle of
John. SBL Dissertation Series Number 33. Missoula,
Mont.: Scholars Press, 1977.

Bornkamm, G.; Barth, G.; and Held, H.J. Tradition and
Interpretation in Matthew. Philadelphia: Westminster
Press, 1963.

Braun, Herbert. "The Problem of a New Testament Theology."
Translated by Jack Sanders. In The Bultmann School
of Biblical Interpretation: New Directions? In vol. 1
of Journal for Theology and the Church, pp. 169-83.
Robert W. Funk, gen. ed. New York: Harper & Row,
1965.

Bultmann, Rudolf. Existence and Faith. Edited and translated by Schubert M. Ogden. Cleveland and New York:
Meridian Books, 1960.

_____. Faith and Understanding. Translated by Louise
Pettibone Smith. Edited by Robert W. Funk. New
York and Evanston: Harper & Row, 1966.

_____. The Gospel of John. Translated by G.R. Beasley-
Murray, R.W.N. Hoare, and J.K. Richer. Philadelphia:
Westminster Press, 1971.

_____. Theology of the New Testament. 2 vols. Trans-
lated by Kendrick Grobel. New York: Charles Scribner's Sons, 1951 and 1955.

_____, and Five Critics. Kerygma and Myth. Edited by
Hans Werner Bartsch. Translated by Reginald Fuller.
New York and Evanston: Harper & Row, 1961.

Christian, C.W., and Wittig, Glenn R., eds. Radical Theology: Phase Two. Philadelphia and New York: J.P.
Lippincott, 1967.

Conzelmann, Hans. An Outline of the Theology of the New
Testament. Translated by John Bowden. New York
and Evanston: Harper & Row, 1969.

_____. The Theology of St. Luke. Translated by Geoffrey
Buswell. New York: Harper & Row, 1960. (German
title: Die Mitte der Zeit.)

Dewart, Leslie. The Future of Belief: Theism in a World
Come of Age. New York: Herder & Herder, 1966.

_____. "God and the Supernatural." The Commonweal
85 (Feb. 10, 1967): 523-28. Reprinted in New Theology No. 5, edited by Martin E. Marty and Dean G.
Peerman, pp. 142-55.

Durkheim, Emile. The Elementary Forms of the Religious
Life. Translated by Joseph Ward Swain. New York:
Macmillan, Free Press, 1965.

Eichrodt, Walther. Theology of the Old Testament. 2 vols.
Translated by J.A. Baker. Philadelphia: Westminster
Press, 1961-67. (The original German edition was
published in 1933-39.)

Evans, Donald. The Logic of Self-Involvement: A Philosophical Study of Everyday Language with Special Refer-

ence to the Christian Use of Language about God as Creator. London: SCM Press, 1963.

Fohrer, Georg. History of Israelite Religion. Translated by David E. Green. Nashville and New York: Abingdon Press, 1972.

Fortna, Robert. The Gospel of Signs: A Reconstruction of the Narrative Source Underlying the Fourth Gospel. London: Cambridge University Press, 1970.

Georgi, Dieter. Die Gegner des Paulus im 2. Korintherbrief: Studien zur religiösen Propaganda in der Spätantike. WMANT, XI. Neukirchen-Vluyn: Neukirchner Verlag, 1964.

Gilkey, Langdon. Naming the Whirlwind: The Renewal of God-Language. Indianapolis and New York: Bobbs-Merrill, 1969.

Hamilton, William. "The Death of God Theologies Today." The Christian Scholar 48 (Spring 1965): 27-48. Reprinted in Radical Theology and the Death of God, pp. 23-50. Edited by Thomas J.J. Altizer and William Hamilton.

Hasel, Gerhard. Old Testament Theology: Basic Issues in the Current Debate. Revised Edition: Grand Rapids, Mich.: Wm. B. Eerdmans, 1975.

Hobbs, Edward C. "An Alternate Model from a Theological Perspective." In The Family in Search of a Future, pp. 25-41. Edited by Herbert J. Otto. New York: Appleton-Century-Crofts, 1970.

_____. "Death and Resurrection ... that Rock was Christ!" motive, April 1956, pp. 14-28.

_____. "A Different Approach to the Writing of Commentaries on the Synoptic Gospels." In A Stubborn Faith: Papers on Old Testament and Related Subjects Presented to Honor William Andrew Irwin, pp. 155-63. Edited by Edward C. Hobbs. Dallas: Southern Methodist University Press, 1956.

_____. "The Ecumenical Movement: Its Theological Spirit." The Perkins School of Theology Journal 7 (Spring 1954): 6-8.

_____. "Gospel Miracle Story and Modern Miracle Stories."
In Gospel Studies in Honor of Sherman Elbridge Johnson, pp. 117-26. Edited by Massey H. Shepherd, Jr.,
and Edward C. Hobbs. Anglican Theological Review,
Supplementary Series (March 1974), no. 3.

_____. The Gospel of Mark and the Exodus. University
of Chicago: Dissertation Series, 1952.

_____. "Norman Perrin on Methodology in the Interpre-
tation of Mark: A Critique of 'The Christology of Mark'
and 'Toward an Interpretation of the Gospel of Mark.'"
In Christology and a Modern Pilgrimage: A Discussion
with Norman Perrin, pp. 79-112. Edited by Hans
Dieter Betz. Society of Biblical Literature, 1971.

_____. "A Theology of the Arts." In The Church, En-
tertainment Media and Moral Values, pp. 6-10. Edited
by Donald Kuhn. Television, Radio, and Film Com-
mission; The Division of Temperance and General Welfare of the General Board of Christian Social Concerns
of the Methodist Church, 1962.

Käsemann, Ernst. "The Problem of a New Testament Theology," New Testament Studies 19 (April 1973): 235-45.

Kaufman, Gordon. God the Problem. Cambridge, Mass.:
Harvard University Press, 1972.

Kümmel, Werner Georg. The Theology of the New Testament
According to Its Major Witnesses: Jesus--Paul--John.
Translated by John E. Steely. Nashville and New York:
Abingdon Press, 1973.

Lonergan, Bernard J. F., S. J. "The Dehellenization of Dogma." Theological Studies 28 (June 1967): 336-51. Reprinted in New Theology No. 5, edited by Martin E.
Marty and Dean G. Peerman, pp. 156-77.

Macquarrie, John. God Talk: An Examination of the Language
and Logic of Theology. New York and Evanston: Harper & Row, 1967.

Marty, Martin E. and Peerman, Dean G., eds. New Theology No. 5. New York: Macmillan, 1968.

Marxsen, Willi. Mark the Evangelist. Translated by R. Harrisville. New York and Nashville: Abingdon Press, 1969.

Matthews, I. G.   The Religious Pilgrimage of Israel.   New York: Harper, 1947.

Niebuhr, H. Richard.   Radical Monotheism and Western Culture, with Supplementary Essays.   New York, Evanston, and London: Harper & Row, 1960.

Ogden, Schubert M.   The Reality of God and Other Essays.   New York: Harper & Row, 1966.

Ogletree, Thomas W.   The Death of God Controversy.   Nashville and New York: Abingdon Press, 1966.

Ramsey, Ian T.   Religious Language: An Empirical Placing of Theological Phrases.   New York: Macmillan, 1957.

Robinson, John A. T.   Honest to God.   London: SCM Press; Philadelphia: Westminster Press, 1963.

Rubenstein, Richard.   After Auschwitz: Radical Theology and Contemporary Judaism.   Indianapolis, New York, and Kansas City: Bobbs-Merrill, 1966.

Schmithals, Walther.   Gnosticism in Corinth.   Translated from the 3d ed.   Nashville and New York: Abingdon Press, 1971.

Schweitzer, Albert.   The Quest of the Historical Jesus.   Translated by W. Montgomery.   With an Introduction by James M. Robinson.   New York: Macmillan, 1968.   Original German, Von Reimarus zu Wrede, published in 1906.   First English edition published in 1910.

Thomas Aquinas.   Summa Theologiae.   Vol 58:   The Eucharistic Presence (3a. 73-78).   Edited by William Barden, O. P.   Blackfriars; New York: McGraw Hill; London: Eyre & Spottiswoode, 1965.

Tillich, Paul.   Biblical Religion and the Search for Ultimate Reality.   Chicago: University of Chicago Press, 1964.

_____.   Systematic Theology.   3 vols.   Chicago: University of Chicago Press, 1951-63.   Phoenix Edition, 1971.

Troeltsch, Ernst.   The Absoluteness of Christianity and the History of Religions.   Translated by David Reid.   Richmond, Va.:   John Knox Press, 1971.   Translated from

the 3d German edition.   Tübingen: J.C.B. Mohr (Paul
Siebeck), 1929.

_____. Christian Thought: Its History and Application.
Edited and with an introduction by Baron F. von Hügel.
New York: Meridian Books, Living Age Books, 1957.
(Original publication, 1923).

_____. "The Dogmatics of the Religionsgeschichtliche
Schule." The American Journal of Theology 17 (January 1913): 1-21.

_____. Der Historismus und seine Probleme. Tübingen:
J.C.B. Mohr (Paul Siebeck), 1922.

Vahanian, Gabriel.   The Death of God.   New York: G. Braziller, 1961.

Van Buren, Paul M.   The Edges of Language: An Essay in
the Logic of a Religion.   New York: Macmillan, 1972.

_____. The Secular Meaning of the Gospel, Based on an
Analysis of Its Language.   New York: Macmillan, 1963.

Vielhauer, Philipp.   "Erwägungen zur Christologie des Markusevangeliums." Zeit und Geschichte.   Edited by Erich
Dinkler. Tübingen: J.C.B. Mohr, 1964.

Vischer, Lukas, ed.   A Documentary History of the Faith
and Order Movement 1927-1963.   St. Louis: Bethany
Press, 1963.

Von Rad, Gerhard.   Old Testament Theology.   2 vols.
Translated by D.M.G. Stalker.   Edinburgh: Oliver &
Boyd; New York and Evanston: Harper & Row, 1965.

Walker, Williston; Handy, Robert T.; Richardson, Cyril C.;
and Pauck, Wilhelm.   A History of the Christian Church.
3d ed. New York: Charles Scribner's Sons, 1970.

Weeden, T.J.   Mark--Traditions in Conflict.   Philadelphia:
Fortress Press, 1971.

Weiss, Johannes.   Jesus' Proclamation of the Kingdom of God.
Edited and translated by Richard Hyde Harris and David
Larrimore Holland.   Philadelphia: Fortress Press, 1971.
(The original German edition was published in 1897.)

Wilckens, Ulrich. Weisheit und Torheit: eine exegetisch-religionsgeschichtliche Untersuchung zu 1. Kor. 1 und 2. Tübingen: J. C. B. Mohr, 1959.

III. Other Works

Benveniste, Emile. "Les classes sociales dans la tradition avestique." Journal asiatique 221 (1932): 117-34.

Dumézil, Georges. Gods of the Ancient Northmen. Edited by Einar Haugen. Berkeley and Los Angeles: University of California Press, 1973.

_____. "La prehistoire indo-iranienne des castes." Journal asiatique 216 (1930): 109-30.

Glachow, Sheldon Lee. "Quarks with Color and Flavor." Scientific American 223 (October 1975): 38-50.

Littleton, C. Scott. The New Comparative Mythology: An Anthropological Assessment of the Theories of Georges Dumézil. Revised Edition. Berkeley and Los Angeles: University of California Press, 1973.

Nambu, Yoichiro. "The Confinement of Quarks." Scientific American 225 (November 1976): 48-60.

Plato. Cratylus. Translated by H. N. Fowler. Loeb Classical Library, Plato Vol. IV.

Skinner, B. F. The Behavior of Organisms: An Experimental Analysis. New York: Appleton-Century-Crofts, 1938.

_____. Science and Human Behavior. New York: Macmillan, 1953; Free Press, 1965.

_____. Verbal Behavior. New York: Appleton-Century-Crofts, 1957.